IN THE KITCHENS OF CASTILE

Papelería de German Herranz
SEGOVIA.
ESTATUA DE JUAN BRAVO.

IN THE KITCHENS OF CASTILE

Gijs van Hensbergen

PALLAS ATHENE

CONTENTS

Opposite: Segovia, the Cathedral, old postcard

Above: *Shepherd and Flock*, by Tom Titherington
Opposite: Segovia, the Aqueduct, old postcard

SEGOVIA. El Acueducto

DUQUE
Con afecto
tu amigo
Cándido

Acknowledgements

To thank all the people who helped with the book and our Segovian adventure would be impossible. The spirit often needed lifting and there were many who on a day-to-day basis provided that support.

Of central importance was the Duque family, who allowed me to work in their kitchens. Pedro Carabias was a wonderful teacher and a glowing example to all the staff. The Martín family of Las Columnas offered even more recipes and friendship. The Prisco family, and Boni and Sagrario, provided a haven for us in our adopted barrio of Santa Eulália. Jai, Soto and José María acted as my third university, and gave me valuable insights into Segovian street life. There were a host of other chefs and shepherds who readily shared their knowledge. I am grateful to them all.

My family played its important part. Ans, Piet, and especially Theo and Alison, gave us enormous support, as did Kirstine Ronnov. It would not be an exaggeration to say that without the help of John and Estelle Coulter, my parents-in-law, this book would not have been possible. They have been wonderful in their generosity.

There were English friends who shared many of our experiences and often helped us touch base: Britt and Annabel, Nick and Josette Bray, Mac and Leslie, Peter Wessel, Marga Lucas and Brenda Gilbert, Paul and Lizzie, Tim and Alexandra. Consistent support and friendship came from Tom and Rebecca Titherington, fellow Segovian adventurers, and neighbours.

The Segovian friends we made meant everything, of course; many of them appear in these pages and all have been essential to the ease with which we were able to make their city our home.

My interest in food, meanwhile, is owed to hundreds of cookery books, but also to the inspiration and guidance of a few special people: Grandma, and Ron and Penny, for the shared meals and hours in the kitchen which taught me how food-making could give much more to life than just sustenance; Katie and Joy Law, who gave more of the same but raised the standards – Marie Singer and Ian Gibson Smith likewise.

Opposite: Duque, from a photograph inscribed for the author

Nicolás

The unfailing enthusiasm of my editor, James Woodall, has been invaluable throughout.

The largest debt is to my wife, Alex, who experienced all the ups and downs but kept going. I can't begin to express what this has meant.

It seems that many books on Spain are tinged with sadness. The memory of Rafael Baixeras and Peli Contreras will always be important to us. More than anything it was their Segovia we discovered.

With this new edition, of course, come new acknowledgements. First in line is Michael Jacobs – hispanist and traveller extraordinaire – who through his writings and sheer force of personality has coloured our interpretation of modern and contemporary Spain. His support and friendship has meant a great deal. Alexander Fyjis-Walker, equally, I am indebted to for supporting this edition. As, too, Jane Bradish-Ellames, my agent

Pedro Carabias and Clemente

at Curtis Brown, who took me on the strength of this book and never lost faith. At Curtis Brown I also thank Euan Thorneycroft for his continued support. For the illustrations I would like to thank Martin Randall and Fiona Urquhart for their kindness in searching out images that show 'ancient' Segovia as depicted by English travellers from centuries ago. And, Tom Titherington, fellow-traveller, touchstone and 'intimo amigo', whose contemporary images of Segovia mean so much to us and to our Segovian friends who all recognise in his depictions the very essence of our shared world.

Laly

for Alexandra

1: To Segovia

Our old 2CV, which had only seen the inside of two garages on the way down through France and Catalonia, crawled painfully up towards the Navacerrada pass. This 2,000-metre-high crossing over the Guadarrama mountains is the shortest route between Madrid and Segovia but in winter, we found out later, to be avoided. Only a week before we had enjoyed a simple New Year's lunch picnic on the beach near Perpignan. Now we were forced to stuff every gap in the doors and windows with coats, blankets and towels in a primitive attempt at insulation. On either side of the car snowploughs had gouged out a deep slushy corridor.

We were as far as we possibly could be from 'sunny' Spain. North, south, east, west, whichever way you went, it was eight hours' drive in a better car than ours to the country's overcrowded beaches. This was supposed to be a different Spain – untouched, abandoned, authentic – where the restaurants served up earthenware dishes of succulent roast meats and pungent stews.

When we reached the top of the pass we looked back south in the direction of Madrid and could still see the immense granite cross that stood guard over Franco's grave, in the 'Valley of the Fallen'. Below us on the other side, just visible through the pine forests and the regiments of skis and sticks, lay Segovia. Beyond Segovia are the flatlands known as the *meseta*, vast plains stretching out for sixty or seventy miles north to the horizon. To the south are the mountains.

The dramatic Guadarrama proves to be an unsurpassable barrier between Segovia and Madrid. The suburban sprawl of the capital that year by year creeps closer to the southern slopes of the Guadarrama has been forced to a halt in the foothills. The great divide is psychological as well. Madrileños look upon the mountains as an area of recreation, a gigantic playground. Segovia is a city that provides entertainment and good Castilian food. For Segovians, however much they might wish to change, the craggy, snow-topped heights mean they will always remain provincial. They are Madrid's poorer cousins. Still, to be a Segovian means a lot to a Segovian – like being one of the chosen race. And after all, Segovia was originally a city and Madrid just a town. Instead of saying that Segovia is close to Madrid, Segovians prefer to have it the other way. As far as history goes there is no competition. Madrid is the brash upstart.

The meeting ground is the mountains. Every weekend the Guadarrama are visited by mountaineers, skiers, mountain-bike aficionados, racing cyclists, ramblers and picnickers, who join together to celebrate the unspoilt and rugged freedom these mountains offer.

If the car had complained so far, it now celebrated its achievement by releasing a series of thunderous explosions as we freewheeled down through hairpin bends. Halfway down, we crossed a small granite bridge that passed high over the raging Eresma river. This, unlikely as it seemed, was supposed to be the setting for Hemingway's *For Whom the Bell Tolls*. What is certain is that for two drawn-out and bloody years during the Spanish Civil War, Franco's Nationalist troops marched up from Segovia to take on the Republicans still holding Madrid. A dreamy and bucolic idyll of pine forests and melting snow, it is now an age away from that bleak chapter in recent history.

The peace and tranquillity were broken at regular intervals by cannon shots from the car that sent sedentary cows and wild horses off on suicidal charges. Shepherds, forests and villagers downed tools and shopping bags to stop and stare; overtaking drivers slowed down alongside us, prolonging the exercise until the next blind corner, just to give the family a better chance to look.

I was oblivious to all. I had my mind fixed on Segovia and one big question: would Cándido, the famous innkeeper of Castile, let me work in his kitchens?

I had already researched and picked up some advance information on Segovia in preparation for my madcap scheme: to work my way up through a Spanish kitchen. Jan Morris has called Segovia the 'city of spirit' after bumping into some sculptures of pigs late one night and running away terrified. It is also home to the world-famous Roman aqueduct striding across one open square to meet the medieval city walls. There are dozens of Romanesque churches, a cathedral, an old Jewish quarter, as well as a fairy-tale Alcázar on which Walt Disney based his castle, and whichever way you look, synagogues, convents, monasteries and palaces. St John of the Cross found the caves under the Alcázar spiritually conducive to the composing of his poems.

All of this pales in comparison with the reputation and fame that Segovia enjoys for producing a hearty and lusty cuisine that knocks any vegetarian straight off his chair. It bears, it is said, the same relationship that nouvelle cuisine does to fish and chips. Nonetheless, Elizabeth David has somewhere written that she enjoyed with relish the cooking of central Spain but couldn't find the time to write about it. Those roasts of suckling pig, milk-fed lamb and wild boar might soon be part of my culinary repertoire. All I had to do was persuade the eighty-five-year-old Cándido that what he really needed in his famous kitchen was an inexperienced art historian with a vocabulary of not more than ten Spanish words.

For the last few miles into Segovia, passing the home of Spain's only home-grown whisky, called DYC, I practiced my speech. It was short and to the point. 'Job. Recipe learn. Write. Famous Cándido. Job. Start now.' That was all there was to it: nothing too long winded, just a few more practice runs and I would have it, word perfect.

'Do you really think you'll get a job working there?' interrupted my wife, Alex, breaking through my train of thought.

'No problem. What's the man got to lose?' With that we coasted past the old bullring into the city of Segovia.

Nothing can quite prepare you for the impact of seeing the Roman aqueduct for the first time on rounding the last sweeping bend. Arch after arch, one on top of the other, marches across the plaza with mesmerising repetition for a hundred yards, dwarfing all the surrounding houses. Despite its construction out of gigantic granite boulders, it has an appearance of remarkable delicacy, as if to ask, 'How did I get through the last 2,000 years?'

The nearest building to the aqueduct is Cándido's. The façade is a mixture of old timber beams, brick and a wonderful old tile roof patterned with dried-out clumps of last spring's moss. The first floor of the restaurant sticks out over the pavement on stilts. Large clouds of smoke were already belching out of the chimney stacks and being blown through the gaps in the aqueduct by the ice-cold wind.

In the window food and made-up dishes were being put on show. Hung up high, the strings of dried shallots, garlic, and two or three types of fiery red peppers were interspersed with bunches of thyme, rosemary, sweet marjoram, a sprig of bay-leaves and other types of herb I couldn't recognize. At either end a pair of wind-dried hams flanked all the other produce. Below, on the cold shelves of the display-cabinet facing the street, a young chef was preparing a display to show off the quality and freshness of the raw ingredients: a fresh salmon, half a dozen trout, a spiny coral pink crab, a side of smoked salmon and a pair of lobsters surrounding a plate of fanned-out salted anchovies; behind them the gaping mouth of a monkfish seemed about to swallow a fresh strawberry gateau. Then the meats: a giant raw steak streaked with creamy fat, a giant lump of the palest pink veal, a plate of tender lamb chops, a pair of pheasants, a string of partridges and a dozen tiny quails. Most striking of all was the strange visual effect of a livid scarlet liver, swelled out almost to bursting, deposited on a silver tray surrounded by the tiny maze-like structures of white lamb's brains speckled with blood.

The chef leant over and added the final details. He lowered a few earthenware bowls of dried-out butter beans into the fridges and pressed in amongst them a red pepper, a bristly pig's ear, a length of curly tail, a black blood pudding and a string of chorizo sausages. On a shelf below the fridge compartment lay jars of green and white asparagus, and a selection of some of the great wines of Spain: a 1968 Gran Reserva Castillo de Ygay from La Rioja, a 1981 Marqués de Arrienzo and, from just north of Segovia, a 1985 Pesquera from the Ribera del Duero – and a bottle of the legendary Vega Sicilia 'Unico', of 1975.

The chef looked out through the window with a mixture of pride and amusement at the interest I was taking in his handiwork. He smiled and busied himself self-consciously with juggling plates and trays a fraction this way, a fraction that. The crab was stood up an inch higher on its powerful claws, the feathers on the partridges were gently stroked down and the salmon slid forward to be nuzzled by the trout. Just as I thought he had finished, with no space left in this exotic still life, he leant back and reached out for the final touch: a leg of lamb and a suckling pig.

The sight of this feast was why I had come to Segovia. Most important of all were the last two items: the suckling pig and the milk-fed lamb.

During the weekends, I had been told, Madrid empties and there are traffic jams of gluttonous city dwellers that stretch back for miles on the other side of the Guadarrama. All the passengers are hunting for the same thing – a good Segovian roast, a couple of kilos of pure protein to keep them going until the next time. Lunches last all afternoon as whole families settle around the heavy oak tables and call out with alarming regularity for just a leg of lamb, or the back half of a pig. One restaurant in Old Castile, rumour has it, has done away with all the niceties and from the moment you sit down a bib is tied around your neck. Knives and forks are dispensed with early on in the proceedings, bringing new meaning to the concept of finger food. Heads lean forward, food goes in, to be washed down with litres of cheap and good rosé. Wanting to eat the food (in an orthodox manner) I saw through Cándido's window was one thing; learning how to cook it was another.

It was time to track down Cándido and deliver my well-oiled speech. After that, when both of us realized the mutual benefit of my suggestion, I could start work. I eyed the produce, as if for mental sustenance, and pushed through the small front door.

Cándido would willingly see me, said the formal head waiter.

'He's waiting for you upstairs.' I climbed up the foot-worn steps and saw Cándido sitting on a high stool behind a tiny little bar. He is an old man who could be taken for one of Franco's brothers. From his full bottom lip drooped an elegant curved pipe, on which he occasionally puffed while riffling through some papers. Over his starched white jacket hung a cluster of medals, the largest of which was from the Chaîne des Rôtisseurs – the French Guild of Master Roasters. After almost sixty years of running the restaurant there wasn't a single award in the Spanish catering business he hadn't won at least once. Behind him on the wall were framed certificates, honours and restaurant reviews, and next to him on the desk was a copy of the menu and copies both of his books, one of which, a collection of his memoirs, is descriptively entitled *I, Cándido*.

I waited until he had finished a line of additions and glanced through the reservations book before launching into my request. I repeated it two or three times but the only glimmer of comprehension on the old man's face was when I said 'Famous Cándido' and 'Recipe learn'. Cándido of course knew what I was after: a copy of his Spanish recipe book. I tried not to give offence but there seemed no way of conveying my message.

Well then, if it wasn't the book I wanted, then another memento of my visit to the Segovian shrine would do: an autographed menu.

It was hopeless. I could see about ten chefs running backwards and forwards through the open kitchen door with baskets and trays of vegetables and meat. He was clearly not shortstaffed. Earlier on in the week we had stopped in the beautiful small city of Cuenca, where the houses cling to the side of the steep cliffs. I had tried the same approach there. The owner of the restaurant had understood me but said with the unemployment being what it was he couldn't let me take work away from a local boy. I tried Cándido for the last time, released my stream of Spanish words in every possible permutation but could see he was getting bored. I thanked him and walked out.

Now what? Alex was sitting in a small patch of sun on the other side of the square admiring the aqueduct. On the steps behind her were two gypsy women with their plastic bags full of lacework waiting to pounce on tourists. She looked happy and excited at being in Segovia. My optimism had proved infectious. No problems, I had told her earlier in the car. 'Within the week we'll be living in Segovia.' It was already proving fractionally more difficult than I had imagined. I would probably meet the same response in every restaurant I went to. Still, it was worth having a look round Segovia.

We strolled slowly up the calle Réal, past an old-fashioned barber who was sharpening his cut-throat razor on a leather strop in the doorway, and the *ferretería* – ironmonger's – with its window-display of kitchen knives, butcher's hooks and brown enamel pans. The patisserie window was full of biscuits, cakes dusted with icing sugar, and buns cut through and stuffed with a mound of cream. Halfway up on the left we passed a restaurant and looked into the fridge in the window. There were bowls heaped high with strawberries and little naked piglets. I peered through the doorway; it appeared to be a smaller version of Cándido's. We walked on following the flow of pedestrians and stopped in a bar whose gigantic picture windows looked out across Mozarabic towers, Romanesque churches and the baked brown tile roofs towards the snow-covered sierra.

Standing at the bar, our feet nestled in the litter of crumpled serviettes, tissue paper, cocktail sticks, cigarettes and discarded food. In the rubbish I could make out mussel shells, heads of prawns, pieces of half-chewed bacon rind, discarded slices of French bread. A woman next to us, between puffs on her cigarette, slipped large gobbets of tripe into her mouth, wiped her lips on a tissue paper and threw it onto the floor. Her partner, a middle-aged business type, with refined features and an expensive suit, stepped back from the bar, growled and hawked his saliva into the sawdust on the floor.

Into our second *café con leche* and individually wrapped stick of sponge cake, we figured there was nothing to be lost by trying the other restaurant we had passed. So I walked back down the hill on my own and in some trepidation entered through the door.

At the far end of the bar in the shadows stood the owner in his white, starched jacket with a bunch of medals hanging round his neck. There was something magical about the interior. Heavy wooden furniture and roof beams, colourful Mexican-style saddle bags and earthenware crocks gave the impression of being caught somewhere in the past, hundreds of years ago – there was even a whiff of the world of Don Quixote. Large legs of cured ham stood on a table, held tightly in a wooden vice, ready for cutting off slices. From the ceiling hung strings of dried red peppers, garlic, smoked chorizo, bunches of dried thyme, rosemary and lavender, and another fifty hams that were finishing off their cure in the mix of thick tobacco smoke and appetizing odours wafting up from the kitchen. On the bar lay a selection of twenty or thirty different tapas, some cold and the others kept warm in stainless steel trays resting in a hot bath of water. There were four different types of olives, salted almonds, a bowl of sunflower seeds, smoked, salted and marinaded anchovies, sardines, *tortilla* (an egg-based potato cake), oven-baked red peppers and pieces of tortilla swimming in a yellow saffron sauce. Looking along the bar there were other dishes to suit every mood and sharpen the appetite: stuffed eggs, slices of Manchego cheese, chorizo, cured pork loin, a dark and forbidding blood pudding, stewed tripe, rings of deep-fried calamaries, squares of salt cod, deep-fried prawns, torpedo-shaped croquettes and spare ribs. There was hardly any space left to put down a glass.

Still, a waiter offered another five dishes, balanced perilously the length of his arm, to the barman who squeezed them into the bar whenever there was space: halved artichoke hearts, meatballs, kidneys in sherry, deep-fried quarters of potato smothered in tomato sauce and a baroque platter of paella. All this food was on offer before even sitting down at table in one of the dining rooms.

I looked around enchanted and had almost forgotten why I was there. Between the cases of awards, cups, medals and commemorative plaques the walls were lined floor to ceiling with photos of the man I recognized as the owner with his arm around famous guests: King Juan Carlos, El Cordobés, Franco, Sophia Loren, Salvador Dalí, Henry Kissinger, a cheerful-looking cyclist, a flamenco guitarist, Queen Sofia, the King and Queen of Greece, and others whose faces rang a bell but I couldn't put a name to. This was obviously a serious place; if I could get a foot in the door I would surely learn something about Castilian cuisine. I then froze as the owner walked towards me and offered his hand.

I decided to use the same introduction as I had with Cándido but dropping the name. I had little option. He looked vaguely puzzled but had a good enough ear for foreign languages to counter my short speech with, '¿Inglés?'

'Si.'

We had made contact. His daughter was called down from the office. Marisa had taken English classes and was keen on Laura Ashley. Not only that, she was also very keen on the trifle that her landlady had made her in Sussex. Would I make it for her? Her favourite was with strawberry-flavoured jelly. If I came to work in the kitchen, would I show the chef how to make it? I answered 'Yes' to all the probing questions. Her father, Dionisio Duque, looked on proudly. The classes had been worth it. The only person we had to persuade was the chef himself. He was called up on the intercom and seconds later he was in the bar.

'Pedro Carabias.'

'Gijs.'

Duque, Pedro and Marisa fired off into high-speed Castilian, and had organized the next few months of my life in a matter of seconds. Another blast down the intercom and Santos, the assistant chef, surfaced. He was young, had the face of a clown, sad, comic and bemused; he offered to be our guide for the first few days. Santos had worked in restaurants on the Costa del Sol and was therefore quite experienced in using sign language. He also had a spare bedroom in his flat and we could move in as soon as we wanted while we looked for a flat of our own. Duque signalled to the two chefs to take me to the kitchens and they guided me down the tight circular stairs from where I could hear the banging of pots and pans, the slamming of doors and the gutsy rasp of Eartha Kitt on the radio.

Pedro was already searching through a locker in the hallway when I reached the bottom of the stairs. Santos called out to the other chefs to come and have a look at *el inglés*. Pedro was giggling as he rummaged through his locker. He pulled out a white jacket and held it up in front of me. I was turned around to model it for the other chefs whose heads were appearing at the door. Santos shouted something unrecognizable from beside the oven where he had taken up his post and they all burst out laughing. The jacket was four sizes too small, designed for someone half my size. Another jacket was tried, but that was no good. Finally, an elegant jacket with the Duque crest was pulled out: it fitted. It belonged to Duque's son Julián, the heir to the throne, a spare that I could borrow. Within five minutes I had been promoted above Pedro Carabias, the head chef, an honorary member of the Duque clan. The next day I had to be back in the kitchen at 8.30 am to start my first proper shift. On our first night Santos offered to show us round.

For the rest of the day our heads swam in a sea of first impressions. Up on the church spires all over the city, storks were busy fetching and carrying, building their nests. We walked down under the city walls in the Eresma valley where the river raged with snowmelt. Along its banks people were already preparing their allotments for the next growing season. And high above we could hear the cathedral bells, the church towers, and the convents and monasteries ringing out the hours and the calls to mass.

Segovia has quite rightly been designated a World Heritage city. Every step you take within the city walls represents a journey into history. Surprisingly, for a city that had been one of the prime movers in the expulsion of the Jews and the Moors, there are still strong echoes of their presence. A large number of the façades are decorated with abstract stucco motifs that must have derived from the strong Middle Eastern influence. One English guidebook claims that Segovia has more Romanesque churches per square mile than any other city in the world. Looking down on the city from a hill on the other side of the valley I could well believe it. Jewish and Arab masons have left an astonishing legacy to the present-day Christians.

Back within the city walls the cobbled streets and alleyways led us past medieval merchant palaces, Romanesque churches, and the restaurants and bars that took up the ground floor of every other building. Everywhere we were met by the sight of suckling pigs resting in the windows;

in one, they had been set up to play football with a cabbage. In the butchers' windows every stage of the food chain could be seen. The busiest shop of all was the offal butcher who proudly displayed what in England would have been hidden out of sight, or minced up into hamburgers and dog food. Suspended from hooks in the marble shrine we could see calves' feet, hearts, kidneys, lungs, intestines, brains, a flared-out face of a calf and a fine purple pair of bull's testicles. The prices were almost as high as for fillet steak. Outside the poulterer's there was a queue of women waiting with enamel pots to take away chickens and rabbits roasted on the spit. The smell on a winter's day was heavenly. At the fishmonger's I could only recognize half of the fish on display and there the business was running at such a pace that customers had to pull out tickets with numbers to keep some sense of order.

For lunch we found a humble little restaurant set in a cave in the old Jewish quarter. The menu of the day was indecipherable but we took it anyway, it was too cheap to argue with. We began with a thick lentil soup that had pieces of ham hock and chorizo in it. A large peasant loaf of bread was put on the table with a litre of red table wine and a bottle of lemonade. It was a warming start to our first Segovian meal and after a long morning's walk the perfect reviver. To follow there was a rabbit stewed in its own vinegar marinade until the meat fell off the bone, accompanied again by more bread to sop up the pungent juice. (At Duque's, Pedro would have to teach me all these dishes.) We stayed at table three full hours and finished with Spanish brandy. We weren't in a hurry and the most important step had been taken.

That evening Santos took us bar hopping and helped us settle in. It was a whole new style of existence and he wouldn't let us pay. With every drink we received a tapa – a small delicacy to accompany an alcoholic drink. It is an artful and sociable method of mixing abstinence with excess, because in every bar we had just one drink and ate just one little titbit. In a bar on the Plaza Mayor we were given a delicious ragout of tuna, onions and tomato on a small round of toast. It was so good I could have eaten another ten, but Santos forbade it. Tomorrow, or the next day, I could have another one, Santos said, as he marched us on to the next bar to taste some squid. In another tiny bar, which twenty customers filled to bursting, the barman had laid out the tapas, Swedish style, on trays for an informal buffet. Santos advised us to take a fino (dry sherry) and then offered us a choice from twenty different dishes. We all went for the same thing, a leaf of endive in which nestled a ball of blue cheese topped off with a smoked anchovy. It was a perfect marriage with the fino, so good that when the barman walked down to the other end of the bar I leant over to help myself. Santos was watching and before my hand reached the dish had clamped his hand round my wrist.

'¡No!' He looked embarrassed and angry.

I tried to pay, but again he refused. He was the first in the bar and so had the right to pay. At the next bar I got through the door first, but that wasn't an adequate excuse for me to reach for my wallet either. Santos was Spanish and would therefore invite us. The etiquette was complicated and his answer was always the same.

'Tomorrow... Mañana... Mañana...' It was pleasing to discover that the legendary *mañana* of Spain could be used for things other than putting off work. Any time in the future I could pay for Santos if I wished but today it was his honour.

It had been an exciting and emotional day. One more bar and then to dinner, Santos suggested, but we were too tired; we needed a bed. I had to start work in the morning. Santos laughed.

'Work tomorrow. Tonight we drink.' But he gave in; the cold winds swept across the plaza and the bars were almost empty.

Pedro was waiting for me in the kitchen and had a broad smile across his face. His eyes were sparkling. He looked at Santos and pointed at his watch.

'Out drinking last night,' he gestured. '¡Mucho! ¡Mucho!' and he hobbled around in a drunken reverie. 'One two three very well fandango. Mucho. Mucho.'

When Pedro smiled his drooping moustache transformed him into a cross between a Mexican bandit and a mischievous faun. His laugh was infectious. The assistant chefs took Pedro's high spirits as a sign to join in. But they read him wrong. He lifted up a sharpening steel and brought it down hard on the bench, shouted their names and gave them their orders. I became 'Gisbert' and we would start with a guided tour.

First the cold room. Crates of vegetables sat on the shelves, giant stockpots rested on the floor, and down the length of one wall there were piglets, lambs and a whole side of beef suspended from hooks.

The kitchen itself was rather old fashioned. In the centre was the large range, with its eight ovens, fuelled by wood and coal. Some of the youngest chefs were already busy stoking it, while others were dragging up sacks of coal, wood faggots and pine cones out of the basement. Mariano, Pedro's stand-in head chef, a human dynamo, had been too busy all this time to throw me anything more than a cursory glance. First he put in the pine cones, followed by the faggots, and then he lit the ovens. The smoke backed up into the kitchen and took a few minutes to clear once the wood had caught. The fire was fed through sets of cast-iron rings that were set into the giant hot plate and by taking them out the heat for the saucepans was regulated from hot to very hot.

Mariano threw in more wood. I was transfixed by the speed at which he got round the kitchen, organizing, shouting commands and stoking the oven; everything was done at running pace and he skated across the floor sliding through the sawdust to get a loaf of bread, a ladle and a saucepan full of milk for our first morning coffee. Nobody had had breakfast and most of us had walked to work in temperatures of -5ºC. The milky coffee was welcome and we took it leaning against the range. There was still no food in sight. Mariano hooked out the cast-iron rings once again, riddled the fire right down and poured on the coals. We were ready to cook.

Pedro stood to one side looking at the reservations list stroking his moustache pensively. I was waiting for my first command. He picked up the intercom and shouted a message to somewhere else in the building and signalled to me to follow him. I couldn't understand a word but figured that the quickest way to learn was to jump, so to speak, straight from the frying pan into the fire.

In the building there were two bars and four large dining rooms, a domed baker's oven for the roast pigs and lambs set deep in the basement, offices and laundry rooms up on the roof. The restaurant could feed 200 or more at one sitting, but January was 'tranquilo', Pedro said. Opposite the kitchen, on the other side of the corridor, was the washing-up room. We walked in and Pedro introduced me to the three washing-up women, who blushed and looked away. Throughout the morning I could see them peeping round the door sizeing me up. What they seemed to like most was when I stood next to Mariano, who only came up to my chest. There were cries of '¡Enorme! ¡Gigante!' that brought the house down. Mariano didn't mind, as he was too busy preparing for the day, and Pedro encouraged the jokes – up to a point. I wanted to help but there was still nothing to do but keep a sharp eye on what was going on around me. There was one young assistant chef who kept winking at me with eyes so baggy that he looked as if he had been born like that. He and his partner had spent the previous hour hauling stock-pans, sacks of wood and produce up into the kitchen. His main interest lay in trying to turn up the volume of the radio gradually on each trip without Pedro noticing. With no common language to resort to, we had joined in a conspiracy to drown the kitchen noises with blasts of heavy metal.

Pedro was ringing round all the fish factors, the middlemen between fishmongers and fishermen, to check out their prices and was placing his orders for the day: salmon, sea bream, monkfish, hake, octopus, mussels, prawns and squid. He gestured me across and gave me an inspection; rolled up my sleeves, tied on an apron and tucked a pan cloth in my belt. Where would I start – alongside Santos making tortillas? With Mariano deep frying circles of squid and fillets of hake? Who would be my master? Perhaps the flat-footed Clemente, a quiet, middle-aged man who hadn't noticed I was there. Clemente was the kitchen's butcher, shy and unassuming. One after the other he hooked up lambs and piglets to a gibbet, and hacked them methodically down the middle with a stainless-steel cleaver. His concentration was absolute. Down they came onto a massive chopping block where he finished quartering them. He was now onto the next stage, smashing up wooden fruit boxes and laying the cross pieces in the bottom of the roasting trays. It was more likely that Pedro would place me alongside Jojo, Fernando and Pototo. They were the *pinches* ('kitchen boys') – the youngest and the lowest in the kitchen pecking order, who were given all the odd jobs and menial tasks. The three of them stood around boxes of vegetables and lettuce, gossiping incessantly as they cleaned, peeled and washed. Pedro had his eye on them and they had theirs on me.

It was clear that Pedro had special plans for me. Marisa walked in and they discussed my training. He was going to take charge of me himself and this way I would learn fastest. I was to be saved, at least, from the back-breaking tasks of coal hauling and dragging round the stockpots. Pedro was happy with the arrangement and ready to teach me. Within a few weeks, I thought, I would have a notebook full of all those authentic Castilian recipes I had dreamed about, Pedro's exclusive information; then, I would be allowed to start cooking for the public as part of the kitchen team. All I needed now was a good set of kitchen knives and a sharpening steel.

I should have bought my own *batterie de cuisine*: a small, general-purpose knife, a larger blade for cutting vegetables, a long flexible one for filleting fish, a good solid chopper, a vegetable peeler and, to show off my assumed prowess, an Italian double-handed mezzaluna for the fine chopping of parsley and all the other herbs I was bound to encounter; a gleaming steak bat, a range of balloon whisks and – the final touch of haute-cuisine sophistication – a melon baller, a pastry brush and a channel cutter for artistic culinary displays.

Pedro was rummaging around in a cupboard under one of the work-tops, obviously looking to kit me up. He would give me my own set of equipment which, so I surmised from my reading in cookery books and catering-trade manuals, I would guard zealously, allowing no one, least of all the pinches, to lay their hands on.

In the hierarchy of the kitchen the tools of the craft are sacrosanct. Chefs travel from job to job taking with them their own set of knives whose properties they come to appreciate with years of handling. Each knife has its particular weight. It has been sharpened down time and time again until its shape and characteristics suit only its owner. Even the handles, some of them bound with Sellotape, have taken the shape of the chef's own hand. These tools, carefully wrapped up in a hessian roll to protect the blades, are his passport to fame.

I was on the point of entering the medieval world of the specialized and secretive guilds where excellence alone was the measure of success. The craft would be an exacting mistress, and unforgiving. Nowhere in Europe had the regional cuisine resisted change and outside influence so strongly as in Castile. Dionisio Duque was the fifth generation in an unbroken line of Castilian innkeepers and his son Julián was waiting in the wings ready to be called on. Over the previous few weeks, travelling through France and Spain, I had come to see this moment as a rite of passage: my first few weeks in Duque's would be a trial by fire, but worth every flame. My knives would be my weapon, my instrument to glory.

There was a loud noise as Pedro upturned colanders, knives, whisks and pans in an effort to root out a spare set of everything for me. At last he found what he was looking for. He replaced his head chef's hat, which had fallen on the floor into the sawdust, and surfaced from under the counter. In his hand he held a camping gaz flame-thrower, the type I had used in London to strip the old paint off second-hand doors. He put it down on the work surface in front of me and lit it. The flame was gradually adjusted until it hissed out a clear blue. With a broad smile creeping across his face Pedro pushed the incendiary device into my hand. I held it out at arm's length as Pedro reached behind me to lift up a sack that had been lying there all morning. Pedro untied the string and, heaving it up, emptied out the contents on the stainless-steel surface in front of me. Santos broke out into a loud and booming laugh. Before me there were hundreds of pig's trotters, ears, noses, tails and pizzles. Pedro showed me how to deal with them. The tails were easy. All I had to do was singe off the hairs. The ears and noses were a bit trickier, requiring a good scrape after an initial torching. It was the trotters that floored me. The smell of burning hoof, flesh and hair was quite overpowering. As I torched away, an acrid and poisonous cloud of smoke enveloped the kitchen. The pinches started coughing and choking. I held my breath and worked on, burning deep into the tight ridges of the trotters' pads. I waited for Pedro to call it a day, but he nodded encouragement. 'Bueno, bueno,' he uttered, and came across to help me with the scraping. Mariano took off his hat, wiped his sweaty forehead on his sleeve and came and leant next to me on the counter.

'Gisbert. ¿Católico?' 'No,' I replied, 'Scottish Presbyterian.' He didn't listen to the answer. 'Atheist,' he announced proudly, striking his chest. Pedro shook his hand up and down.

'Mariano, muy mal, mal. ¡Malisimo!'

'¡Communista!' Santos chipped in.

With Pedro and Mariano's help the pile grew smaller. It was a speciality of the region, Pedro told me. Perfect, I thought; this would really catch on back in England. Should I take notes? Pedro was insistent. It was a typical winter dish: butter beans with pig's parts – *judiones de la Granja*. He would show me how to make it another day; today, something easier.

One by one the waiters were coming in to have their lunch. Mariano had prepared a thick stew of potatoes and lentils, followed by a plate of pork fillet steaks and deep-fried green peppers. The laundry girl and washer-uppers sat down at table with them and started to eat. We, the chefs, would take ours later.

When I wasn't working, Alex and I spent our time flat hunting, and looking for a job for her. At four o'clock every afternoon, when the worst of the lunchtime rush was over, we waited in a bar on the Plaza Mayor and kept our eye on the kiosk for the delivery of the daily edition of the local paper. Santos's flat was central but we couldn't encroach on his hospitality for too long. Our bedroom overlooked the calle Réal and after the first weekend we discovered why Santos had chosen the back bedroom, instead of ours with its view. On Friday night we were kept awake until four with the late-night bar hoppers. On Saturday it was the same and Sunday was worse. Early one evening we had joined a *paseo* – procession – up and down the calle Réal. All the families were out: the mothers immaculately dressed in their expensive furs and jewels, the fathers in suits and ties, and the children in their best party frocks and suits.

Below our window the paseo wandered slowly up to the Plaza Mayor. Every so often it ground to a halt as family and friends met, and children showed off the presents they had received a few days earlier, 6 January, the day of the Three Kings. Despite the bitter cold, there was a festival atmosphere in the air.

In the Plaza Mayor, the *tuna* – a band of travelling minstrels – moved from bar to bar playing traditional Segovian songs. On one side of the square, the steam was rising up from the churros man's giant cauldron of boiling oil. A long queue had formed to buy his deep-fried doughnut sticks, which were then taken into the bars and eaten with thick hot chocolate.

By 10 pm the square had almost emptied and we were expecting a good night's sleep. It was only the beginning. Slowly the plaza started filling up again as the city's youth prepared to hit the discos. We settled ourselves in an old bar in the Jewish quarter and watched the revellers. The interior was eccentric and old fashioned. The decoration consisted of budgerigar cages, their occupants chirping away, and the ceiling was burnt a deep brown with years of tobacco smoke and soot. In one corner sat the ancient landlady busy with her crochet. Occasionally she looked up to throw another log in the fire and shout advice to her husband, who was despatching the drinks. After a few minutes we were joined at the table by the first in our collection of Segovian eccentrics, Forty-Eight Hours (as we later called him).

He invited himself to a drink and settled on his stool. He was in his mid-thirties with a gaunt and weathered face, and surprisingly for the time of year wore only a T-shirt. With his small command of English he recounted his story. He was very keen on England, but after a disastrous first trip he would never go back. It was a wonderful country, he insisted, but – he sweated nervously at the memory of his stay. On the plane, he explained, frightened by the flight, he had overdone it on the miniatures. By the time he reached Heathrow his coordination had gone and he needed helping off by the police. He put up a good struggle, but after smashing a plate-glass window in the arrivals' lounge, he found himself in a cell. For forty-eight hours he remained locked up and was put on the next plane to Madrid. Despite it all he still loved England, 'particularly its sense of tradition'. His friendliness towards us and anything English, however, was mitigated by an undisguised propensity to order himself drinks on our account. It was getting late, so we cut our losses and ran. It was two in the morning and the bars were still full. I thought about Duque's, but we stayed out till the end.

ALCAZAR AT SEGOVIA.

2: Two weeks later

Two weeks later we were installed in a flat of our own. It had to be restored and redecorated but otherwise it was ideal. The bedrooms were tiny dark caves set off the main rooms, typically Moorish in design: warm in winter and cool in summer. Facing onto the market street below there was an elegant glass balcony with decorative ironwork. From there we could see the snow-topped sierra and look across into the gardens of the military academy. Two floors below we had a butcher, a tobacconist, a pharmacy, a button shop, a newspaper stand, a vegetable and fruit stall, and the most authentic bar in town. It was a tiny, self-enclosed enclave – a barrio within a barrio. When business was slack the shopkeepers would stand in the street chatting to each other. And if there was bullfighting or football on the television in the bar they would take it in turns to keep their eye on the shops.

The man in the newspaper stall looked sad and depressed. At lunchtime all the shopkeepers would sit in their groups and share a tin of sardines, a bag of olives, or an improvised salad cut onto a plate, borrowed from behind the bar. It would always be the same group at the same table. But the newspaper man lived in a different barrio, five minutes' walk away. He was a loner. He sat next to me at the bar. He was victimized by the traffic passing inches from his window and the memory of a lorry dragging his shop a few inches up the street the previous year played on his nerves. We would have to watch out, he warned us, and make sure that we kept all our doors locked. There were bad people about – 'chorizos,' he called them.

After a few days he plucked up the courage to ask us for our help. He had noticed that from our balcony we could see his shop. Would we keep an eye on it at night and if anything suspicious happened would we immediately phone the police? Of course, I said, but we don't have a phone. It didn't matter, the most important thing was that he could trust us to guard it, while he sat at home worrying. The following afternoon on my way back from Duque's I stopped off to buy the local paper. He was extremely agitated.

'Did you phone the police last night?' I felt a pang of guilt. Had we failed him on our first night as unofficial security guards? I hadn't heard or seen anything – nobody breaking in, no vandals, no lorries ramming his shop. What had happened, I asked? 'Nothing!' He was just making sure we were doing our job.

Once we had settled into the flat properly our landladies Sagrario and Boni asked us up for dinner. It was a special occasion. A bottle of sparkling cider had been opened and we were invited to sit at the round table. Under it was an electric heater, and the thick tablecloth that fell down to the ground was picked up and wrapped tightly around the waist. During the cold winter months all social life, mending chores, knitting and crocheting were centred around this table. It was an effective system. We were ordered to take the best seats while Sagrario and Boni laid out the supper in front of us. It was a simple meal: green beans with burnt garlic, fried slices of spicy chorizo and a large, round tortilla. They were happy we had taken the flat. It had been empty for sixteen years, but they hadn't really thought of renting it out again. It was the sight of my pleading wife that persuaded them.

During the meal I saw their eyes focusing on Alex's wedding ring. How long had we been married? Were we going to have children here in Segovia? Little segovianos? It would be healthy to bring them up here rather than in a large city. The air was good. Alex was force-fed in preparation for the great day. More tortilla. Finish off the chorizo. Some more bread. Her labour was imminent. Whenever I was brought into the conversation it was merely as an appendage to my wife, a diversion. I must look after her well. Keep her warm in winter. She was beautiful, they told me. I was fat and ugly – not meant, I like to think, as an insult. It was just that my wife's star had to shine brighter – quite rightly, in their view. I had obviously made a very good catch. Whenever the conversation flagged, Sagrario jumped in with a machine-gun eulogy:

'Alejandra. Alejandra. Alejandra. Alejandra.' She would pinch her cheek, stroke her hair and give her a cuddle. Sagrario had found a new sister. We must come round whenever we wanted, and not just on rent day, like all the other tenants. Whatever we needed we had to ask them for.

The following morning on my way out the door I bumped into them both in the downstairs hall. Armed with buckets, mops and bags of cleaning fluid they were on the way up to clean our flat. It was just as well I was going to work because they had the morning free to be with Alejandra, and they would teach her how to wax the red tile floors, clean the windows and take her shopping. As a newly-wed in their Segovia, she had a lot to learn.

I had taken the previous day off to sort out the bureaucracy of renting the flat: a visit from the health inspector, contracts to be signed and the electrician had come round to finish off the rewiring. The electrician was as strict as everyone with respect to siesta. At two he knocked off for lunch and wouldn't be back until five. By the time he returned the flat was dark. No matter: he finished off his work with a torch strapped to his head. For the first time that night we would have some form of heating, and could sit down and read a book.

'We thought you'd gone on holiday,' shouted Santos on my return to Duque's. 'Off to Benidorm, to lie on the beach.' Pedro shuffled in dragging a stockpot full of judiones de la Granja.

'You still work here, then? Come on, give me a hand. I'll show you some of the simple dishes.' Pedro prepared coffee and we leant against the counter, dipping our sponge cake. He pulled out his wallet. He showed me his identification card. His birthday was on 23 February, the same day that Colonel Tejero's coup attempt on the Cortes (the Parliament in Madrid) failed back in 1981 – a double cause for celebration. On that night, opposite our flat in the military academy, the tanks and armoured cars, we were told, had kept their engines running hour after nervous hour in case of an emergency while they waited to see the outcome of Tejero's harebrained daring.

Pedro was born in the village of Chañe, north of Segovia, out on the open plains. His brother worked as the maître d' in Cándido's and that's where Pedro had done his training under the legendary Tomás Urrialde. His cousin, Primitivo Martín, who owned a bar called Las Columnas off the Plaza Mayor, was another of this friendly mafia of chefs that hailed from his village. Urrialde, known to all as the Mushroom Man due to his expertise in that art, had trained them all. They were like one big family, Pedro told me. They still sometimes, when they had time, went out together but now that they were all married their real families inevitably took pride of place. Being a chef was hard work and Pedro, still only in his early forties, already had trouble with his back. It was an occupational hazard. All those stockpans that needed hauling up the stairs and the hours on your feet made for an unhealthy life. 'Just wait until the summer,' Pedro warned me, 'and then see how hot it gets in here.'

Pedro pulled out a photo of his wife and family. He was a proud father. His son was already up to grade eight on the piano, and his daughters spoke a good basic English and were preparing to go off to Madrid University. His life in Segovia's kitchens had made it all possible, and although he didn't say it, I sensed the last place he would want any of his children working was behind a restaurant range.

The kitchen was in that fallow period between the preparation of all the tapas and the 'family' lunch, and the hectic moment the first clients started coming in. It was the eye of the storm. Clemente stood in his corner close to the chimney stacks stealing sips from his coffee cup and chewing on a fresh pork scratching as he watched my progress with seeming indifference. He worked on quietly without a break, bending down low to pull roasting trays filled with piglets and lambs out of the bottom ovens as he basted them to perfection. His concentration was never far away from the state of the fire – it was his most basic and effective tool, and he was a slave to its whims.

He tended to steer clear of the kitchen gossip except when he was the subject of the joke, and Santos made sure that was as often as possible. Clemente had the unfortunate luck to live in a farming village a few miles out of Segovia. So, according to Santos, he couldn't really be thought of as a chef, more a peasant. Anyway, Santos swore on the Virgin that one day he had seen Clemente coming in to work on a tractor with his sheep and dogs running behind. Santos pulled Clemente's hat down over his eyes and they started to wrestle.

'Basta,' shouted Pedro, and they stopped. Everyone laughed. Clemente's station in the kitchen, as butcher and roaster, meant his break came later, at around 3pm. That was when Santos, Pedro and Mariano would be working flat out keeping up with the orders: steaks, omelettes, prawns in garlic, asparagus with mayonnaise, frogs' legs and a host of other dishes.

Mariano came and joined us. Perhaps I could give him a few classes in English during the afternoon break? I didn't see why not. The news spread like wildfire. By the end of lunch I had two further clients for my improvised class, a waiter and the maitre d', and every single female in the building from the laundry girl down. They had all been inspecting me from a discreet distance over the last few weeks, so I took it as a compliment. After Sagrario and Boni's bashing, I could do with the lift.

Mariano was keen to see the world and English might come in useful. He was one of eight children and had worked his way up the kitchen ladder fast; he had had to. He never stayed working in one place long, just enough to save some money to go off on his travels. When they needed him they called him, and there was always weekend work cooking for banquets and weddings. During the spring that meant almost every day. He was a keen mountaineer, and all his free days were taken up with altitude training and the testing of his equipment. Sometimes, after a long day in the kitchen, he would take his tent up the mountain and sleep in the snow. The next morning he'd be in bright and early. He had just come back from scaling Mount Kenya, so he had to start off again from scratch, with nothing in the bank. His next plans were for a Himalayan expedition, hence his working every single shift. Earlier in the morning he had been interviewed by the local radio station, we had all had our ears glued to the set.

'Did you know that Clemente's village has been put into quarantine?' asked Santos. 'It's true. The woodworm has got through half the village already. Clemente's all right though, they won't go near him. The only thing you'll have to watch out for' – turning round to Clemente – 'is to put your pipi away in your trousers.' Another battle started but it fizzled out soon enough. They were the best of friends, after a fashion.

Duque walked in. He shook my hand, formally. Was I learning a lot? Was I happy in my work? Marisa was still waiting for her trifle. He had never tried it himself and would also like a taste. It might even go on the menu. I didn't think so. I made my excuse; the jelly still hadn't arrived from England. I needed a special flavour, they only had lemon in the supermarket.

'Pedro,' Duque announced with gravity. 'Today we have some very distinguished guests from the military academy: three generals and two other members of staff. I want the best suckling pig in the house prepared al punto for exactly a quarter to four.' Pedro nodded and Clemente obeyed. 'Don Gisbert. Today you can witness the ceremonial carving of the pig for which we are famous throughout Spain.'

Over the last few weeks I had been doing my homework on Duque's, talking to people, checking in books and looking through cookery magazines. Wherever Cándido's appeared, Duque's was alongside. A strong rivalry existed between the two restaurants, particularly as a few generations back the families had been related. It was good for Segovia. Rumours abounded. One was for the Yankies, the other for the Japs. One was for the Spaniards, the other for the Segovians. Everyone had his favourite, where they served the best lamb, the best pig, the most generous portions, the best tapas, had the friendliest barmen, the prettiest ceremonial ladies, the best style, the best air-conditioning and so on *ad infinitum*. A Segovian, I was beginning to learn, when brought round to the subject of food, was never short on opinions. Social life was conducted in the restaurants and bars, and not in the home, so the setting was important.

The best business for most of Segovia's top-rung restaurants were the various institutions: the banks, the local building society, the military, the town council and the local government. When the foreign tour groups and the Madrid weekenders fell off during the winter, these could still be relied upon. They merited the best attention, because they were the most discerning of the clientele and also paid the rent.

When the time came for the ceremony Duque would call. The kitchen set to work. Pedro was going to teach me how to make a proper *tortilla.*

2 large floury potatoes *Salt*
Half an onion *4 to 5 eggs*
Olive oil

Peel and slice the potatoes. In a frying pan pour in enough olive oil to cover the potatoes. Don't skimp. The oil is later drained off and used for the same purpose again. Fry the potatoes in the oil until tender and halfway through add the diced onion. The oil should cook the potatoes but not be so hot that they brown. Drain and reserve the oil. Wait a minute for the potatoes to lose heat and in a mixing bowl add the beaten eggs to them. Season with salt. Pour into a non-stick pan and cook for ten minutes on a gentle heat. Cover with a plate, turn over and slide back in. Another ten minutes and serve.

When Pedro demonstrated he flipped over the thick tortilla like a pancake. I could practice the movement, he suggested, at home with dried chickpeas, with a forfeit for every one that fell out. Otherwise, the plate was the most reliable method. The art of making the perfect tortilla, Pedro explained, was that it should be cooked through, yet still good and moist. Every Spanish housewife knew how to do it. It was easy. Pedro searched through a drawer to find an old recipe cuttings book he had used since he was a pinche. He pulled out a recipe from Madrid during the 'Hunger Years' in the fifties. It was for a 'potato tortilla' – so it was entitled – devoid of potatoes, eggs, olive oil and onions. The culinary miracle relied on the cook's ability to transform orange zest, flour and water into something resembling the same. Pedro had never tried it. Chañe, the village where he spent his youth, was overrun with chickens and ducks.

Pedro was in a teaching mood. I had paid for the class with close on a month of unexciting chores: stripping artichoke leaves, peeling a thousand garlic cloves, beating eggs, lifting stockpots and, not without a degree of self-interest, religiously collecting our lunchtime pitchers of wine. Communication was beginning to be less of a problem, though many of the words the waiters and pinches taught me were unrepeatable outside the kitchen. I was interested to find out that on the obscenity scale, the sexual expletives were the least likely to give offence. If I let one out within earshot of the washer-uppers they barely blanched.

When my education moved on to those with religious connotations, however, the cries of horror crossed the landing. The very worst was the host – *hostia* – the sacramental wafer. Pedro forbade it, unless exceptional circumstances demanded it. It was good for a pan fire, for example, a serious burn or a cut with a knife, but very little else. I guarded my tongue carefully. The waiters had already set me enough linguistic traps. At home with a dictionary I had to cross off large areas of the vocabulary I had so laboriously learnt. But Pedro was forgiving and laid the blame at the right door. Next week, he suggested, on his only day off, it would be an honour if I would come with my wife for dinner at home and meet all his family. My Spanish was clearly becoming more than passable.

'What do you think of Castilian food?' one of the barmen asked me. 'Better than English, no?' Different, I replied. 'All the friends I know who have visited England just can't understand it. There's no wine. No bread and no chorizo. A gigantic breakfast and dinner at six. It doesn't sound healthy. And sometimes, they told me, they were only given sandwiches for lunch.' He paused. 'Is it true you put everything on the same plate? The meat, the potatoes and the vegetables?' It obviously worried him. 'You ought to come home and try my mother's cocido, it's the absolute best. *¡Muy rico!*' It's a wonderful dish, I agreed, but it's one with meat, potatoes and vegetables, like any other stew. 'Yes, but you don't eat it all at once. It was a matter of style and an hour-long lunch followed by a siesta is difficult to beat. 'Jamón de York is not as good as Spanish ham. Admit it.' 'It's not, but then it isn't from York. It's from Spain.' He looked perplexed. 'Well, what's your favourite Castilian dish? Cochinillo [suckling pig] or *cordero* [milk-fed lamb]?' My general answer to this is that they're both very good, but I personally can't eat cochinillo too often; it is just too rich. Cordero is another story; it is exquisite. There is so much variety in the way you can cook it.

And many of the tapas are absolutely wonderful: for instance, the red peppers and a garlic-laden dish of mushrooms. Pedro was breathing over my shoulder.

'Shall I teach you?' Of course.

½ kg mushrooms
3 cloves garlic
Teacup chicken or beef stock
1 tbsp chopped parsley
Squeeze of lemon
2 tbsp olive oil
Salt

Slice the garlic cloves and fry in the oil until golden. Scoop out and reserve. Clean and quarter the mushrooms and fry until they take colour. Add the stock and reduce to half. Season with salt, lemon, and sprinkle with the fried garlic and parsley. Serve.

In a normal household this is normally prepared in a frying pan, but in the restaurant it was different. For many of the garlic-flavoured dishes we used small, flat earthenware bowls. After months of use they become tempered enough to take the highest heat. If they occasionally break it doesn't matter, as they are so cheap. They are placed straight onto the hot plate and used as a primitive but highly effective frying pan.

This is the method Santos also used to prepare the prawn speciality – *gambas al ajillo*. It was even simpler than the mushrooms. He threw the garlic and a red-hot pepper into the oil and a few seconds later the prawns; then an addition of lemon and parsley, and it arrived on the customers' table still spitting away. The most dramatic of all, and the gourmet's favourite, was a dish of *angulas* – baby eels. The waiter was told to get ready. The spaghetti-like elvers were thrown in the garlic- and pepper-flavoured oil, the dish was quickly covered with a saucer and the waiter sprinted to the table. You could hear the waiter shouting his warning to oncoming traffic of '*¡Voy! ¡Voy! ¡Voy!*' as he scaled the narrow staircase two floors above.

The intercom buzzed. A garbled message came through. I figured that the day I could catch the sense of more than fifty per cent of what was going on I would be well on the way to mastering castellano. Duque wanted me to get ready for the ceremony and smarten up a bit for presentation.

The perfect piglet was lifted out of the oven and laid on an earthenware dish, a barque, nestling on branches of thyme. The flame-thrower was lit and the conchinillo toasted a deep golden brown. Duque called down, and Pedro and I walked up in procession, the piglet held on high. In the top dining room, Duque was waiting for us at the general's table, A bottle of Vega Sicilia was being opened for them, but all eyes had focused on the splendid cochinillo. Pedro put it carefully on a side table and Duque took up his position alongside. The thyme was lit and burst high into flame. It was pure showmanship. Duque waited for the flames to die down. Around his neck and pinned to his jacket were more medals than the generals' put together. He picked up a plate and cleared his throat.

'Esteemed guests, as Master Roaster of Castile and member of the select organisation of the Chaîne des Rôtisseurs, I present in your honour the finest cochinillo in all of Old Castile. For five unbroken generations my family has developed and perfected the exquisite roasting of corderos and cochinillos for which we are justly famous.' It was not clearly, a moment, for modesty, rather for the skilful arts of diplomacy and publicity, the crowning moment of Segovian culinary and civic pride. Duque lifted the plate high above his head. 'In the style of the famed Master Roasters who served at the court of Henry IV of Castile and witnessed by our distinguished chef who has come all the way from England to learn the secrets of our trade, I will now carve you the cochinillo.' Two months earlier I had in fact been making egg-mayonnaise rolls in Covent Garden, but I wasn't going to correct him now.

The plate was brought down fast. With four stabbing blows Duque had carved the cochinillo perfectly, using nothing more than the blunt edge of a plate. Pedro looked satisfied. The crackling, as fragile as porcelain, had split clean down the middle and the heady perfume of the flesh was released. This was a dish for serious eaters. Duque waited a moment longer and with an actor's sense of timing threw the plate crashing to the floor. It shattered in a hundred pieces – one piece for every year of good luck. Pedro tapped me on the shoulder.

'Come on, let's get cooking.' We turned to go. But Duque didn't miss this last chance for theatre. He swept out his arm with proprietorial authority and gestured us away.

'Pedro! Gisbert! To work! To work! We have hundreds more clients waiting. There is no time to lose.' The generals were impressed. They appreciated a man who could give out the orders. 'The cochinillo is tender, no?' The trenchermen nodded in approval. Duque addressed me gravely. '*Riquísimo*. Succulent. Exquisite. You have learnt something today, Don Gisbert.'

The lunchtime rush was winding down. Clemente rested up against the stove and chewed a roll. The last job of all was to prepare the Duques' family lunch. Marisa usually wandered down mid-morning to discuss it with Pedro. What was the best fish? Could he do something with pasta? They ate in the restaurant every day, so they often asked for something different or out of the ordinary, to ring the changes. Like all traditional Spanish families, they met over the table.

The afternoons were generally quiet, without the mad minute-to-minute panic of meeting the orders rushed down by the waiters. It was then that we prepared some of the advance dishes for the following day: the pâtés, a vegetable terrine, the oven-baked red peppers, *chorizo en olla*, marinaded pork tenderloin, partridge in *escabeche* and creamed rice pudding. After four o'clock the fires were riddled out and left to burn down slowly. For the chefs, the worst was over. Before the ovens lost too much heat Pedro and Mariano would make cakes and sponge puddings, and once they had gone out the pinches, as part of their penance, could look forward to the most horrible job of the day, the scrubbing of the hot plate. It was the one job I fortunately never had to do. Pototo and

Fernando would lean over the still warm range and, armed with caustic soda and a pumice stone, grind away for quarter of an hour trying to bring the surface back to its original shine. On a freezing cold day it looked just about bearable but in the summer it would be a nightmare. Santos whipped them on. Sweating away, the two of them worked backwards and forwards until it had met with Pedro's approval. It was the one time of the day that their sense of humour completely failed them.

Clemente stood idly to one side. He had worked eight hours without a break and looked exhausted. He opened a deep drawer and pulled out a few large round loaves of stale white bread. He cut them up with a razor-sharp knife into gobbets. I thought maybe he had a passion for birds and was going up on the roof to feed them – but no. The bread was for eating and was going to be used tomorrow for a large group of tourists in the traditional sopa castellana. I didn't fancy anyone's chances if they wore false teeth, but Pedro assured me it was right. It was a life-sustaining peasant dish, just the thing for a winter's day. I found it hard to believe.

I pulled off my jacket and put it into Pedro's locker. We were all ready for a break. I walked up the stairs and Mariano shouted behind me.

'Watch out for your wife tomorrow. It's the fiesta of Zammaramala and the women run the village for a day. It might give her ideas.' He laughed.

I walked down the calle Réal with Pedro. We bumped into his brother from Cándido's, who was with another brother. He was in a happy mood; he was taking a couple of days' holiday, still owed to him from well before Christmas, and his was going back to visit his village. It was only forty kilometres away but he hadn't been back there for almost a year. Out in the country it was too cold in the winter and the boredom was terrible. There wasn't enough work left for everyone and that's why as a young man he had moved into the city. Peasant life was very, very hard.

'Don't bother coming in tomorrow,' Pedro said, 'go to the fiesta. Anyway, it's a special year. Duque's going to be the good man in the celebrations. Or is it the bad man? I can't remember. It was on the radio this morning.'

The next morning we walked to Zammaramala following the old medieval city walls. It was a beautiful crisp morning and in the shade of the walls there were still patches of snow to be seen. High above us, perched on the rock, was the formidable Alcázar – a mishmash of different styles and periods of restoration. Before the 1860's it had been used as the military academy but then caught fire. Apparently the arsonists were the trainee soldiers who, bored to distraction with Segovian nightlife in those pre-disco days, razed it to the ground. They had then hoped for a transfer to Madrid but were frustrated in their plans. Instead, they were moved up to the street where we lived: calle de la Muerte y Vida – Death and Life Street.

The fertile market garden below the Alcázar was steeped in legend and history. Up in the caves above us was where St John of the Cross had scratched out his hermitic existence, writing down his strange mystical meditations. A hundred yards further up the hill was the twelve-sided Crusader church of the Vera Cruz – a delightful example of Knights Templar architecture. Every year, the guard told me, on Good Friday, the Order of Malta who had inherited it from the disbanded Templars flew in from all around the world to partake in their ancient ritual.

The strangest of all the legends and miracles attached to this part of the Eresma valley was that of Mary of the Somersaults. In the last years of the fifteenth century, under the rule of Ferdinand and Isabella, Segovia suffered from an orchestrated and brutal period of Catholic intolerance. The Jews and Moors, who made up more than half the city's population, were ordered to convert or move on. It was considered a total success. But a few years later doubt started to creep back into the Catholic community. What if the Moors and Jews who had converted to Catholicism were really only just pretending? When was the last time that anyone had seen either Mohammed or Ishmael – or for that matter Mary – tucking into jamón serrano or salivating over a large earthenware platter of succulent cochinillo? Had anyone seen them in church lately? The mood of the Catholics grew ugly. It was obvious. The converts were a bunch of fakers. A test case would have to be made, an example set. And Mary was chosen.

An angry crowd marched Mary to the Alcázar and threw her off the cliff. She somersaulted through the air, faster and faster, until she almost hit the ground. But suddenly she stopped. An angel had flown in and caught her, lowering her gently down onto her feet in the meadow below. The crowd cheered. It was a miracle. Mary was renamed Fuencisla – a common Segovian girl's name – and a shrine built to the Image of the Fuencisla in commemoration of the angel that had flown in to save her.

Centuries later, during the first year of the Spanish Civil War, General Francisco Franco heard of the story. He needed someone like Fuencisla as a member of his staff. In a solemn military ceremony, with hundreds of officers and lower ranks present, Fuencisla was promoted over their heads into a full field marshal, and equipped with a baton and sash. Hitler only met Franco once and that experience, he claimed, was like having a tooth pulled out without anaesthetic. When he heard about Fuencisla he vowed never to meet him again.

Down by the shrine the crowds were growing fast. Coaches were pouring in from all over Spain. Today's fiesta, Pedro had told me, was going out live on national television. Over the last few years the feminist movement had latched onto the Zammaramala festivities as a symbol of the future and it made for good publicity.

The story behind the fiesta was almost as dramatic as that of Mary of the Somersaults. Back in 1085, Segovia was still the frontline of the war between the Moors and Christians. Zammaramala, just half a mile up the hill, had fallen to the Christians. But the Moorish Alcázar held out long against the siege. From the front it was unbreachable and the strength of the garrison force was unknown. How could it be taken?

The women of Zammaramala, famed for their outstanding beauty, to say nothing of their cunning, marched down the hill to dance in front of the castle walls. Knowing that the Latin temperament does not stop at the Straits of Gibraltar, they bared their breasts to tempt the heathen Moors out of their rocky stronghold, thus giving their menfolk enough time to get in through the back door of the Alcázar. Segovia was won for the Christians. Unfortunately for the women their breasts were cut off by the deceived Moors; and to this day the patron saint of the village is the Sicilian martyr St Agatha, who in the third century suffered a similar fate after rejecting the advances of a Roman prefect.

In recognition of their bravery, each year two women of the village are voted 'mayoresses' and run the show for the day. This year it was María Manso and Fele Velasco, the local plumber's wife. By the time we walked up the hill the village was heaving. There were only three official bars in the village but anyone with the smallest degree of entrepreneurial spirit had transformed their patio and garage into a makeshift bar. The choice was limited to chorizo and wine, but that was significant, because the women of the village and the 'mayoresses' would later be feasting on the same in the village town hall.

No men were allowed at the lunch, except the priest. He was requested to wear his cassock, which looked more like a skirt, and was refused any of the hard stuff. His lunch would be a cup of hot chocolate and sponge cake. The women were firmly in the driving seat but, on first appearances, most of the village menfolk had escaped from their chores and countered feminine guile with male necessity. They were either propping up the bars or working hard behind them.

The Duques drew up in their Mercedes, which was parked away safely in the Mayor's garage. Along with Alfredo Matasanz, the director of the local radio station, Dionisio Duque was a guest of honour, chosen for his good works in the previous year in the promotion of local tourism. They had arrived just in time. Fele Velasco was pushing through the crowds on her way to collect her fellow 'mayoress'. She looked wonderful in her colourful local costume. On her head she wore an eccentric and heavily worked tricorn hat with a pompom on top. Over her tight-fitting black velvet jacket she had thrown an intricate lace paisley pattern shawl. The outfit was finished off with a wide, sweeping skirt, and an abundance of gold and red coral jewellery, the family heirlooms. Fele and María joined up with their assistants and strode on to the church.

There they picked up the small wooden statue of St Agatha and raised it on their shoulders. In her hand, St Agatha held out a tray, on which lay the silver effigies of her breasts. The procession was about to begin. The small band struck up and the assistants of the 'mayoresses' started a swirling dance down the main street. Some of them carried halberds that were supposed to have been captured from the Alcázar. They danced in pairs, with their hands circling and twisting above their heads in intricate patterns; each dancer concentrated on matching the complicated footwork of her partner. The priest and the 'mayoresses' followed, bringing up the rear. The spinning dancers led us on until the moment we could have been spotted clearly from the ramparts of the Alcázar. They turned back and returned to the church for mass. There was no room to squeeze into the church, so we used the break in the festivities to sample more rosé and chorizo. Everyone was in high spirits but no one was drunk, except for one old crimson-faced codger, but he looked as if he hadn't been sober since the day his mother dipped his dummy in the local anise. We spotted Forty-Eight Hours but then lost him in the crowd. A coach tour of Japanese looked on in puzzled admiration as the procession trooped out of the church to the main square for the final acts.

Suspended above our heads from a hangman's noose was a masked scarecrow effigy of Everyman, constructed out of straw. It was the moment for the women s revenge. Duque and Matasanz were joined by the other major participants on an old stone drinking trough in the middle of the square. A local bard sang their praises in rhyming couplets to the cheers and boos of the assembled mass. The awards were given out and then the straw effigy was doused with petrol and set alight by Fele and María. The crowd pushed back as the victim exploded into flame. Zammaramala's womenfolk cheered and marched the priest off to his banquet of baby food.

It was back to the bars again. Visitors had brought packed lunches and set them out on any spare tables in the bar. Tortilla rolls were taken out of their silver foil, Wiener schnitzels laid out on plates and husbands sent to the bar to order drinks. Tins of anchovies, stuffed olives and marinaded mussels were peeled open. One of the sons carved hunks of bread off a giant loaf with a clasp knife.

'*Que aproveche*,' I intoned – enjoy your meal. And they invited us to sit down and share their lunch. We declined their offer out of courtesy – it was a Spanish formality.

On our way down the hill I was accosted by Fele and María.

'Please, give us some money' – and they howled with laughter. 'We need it to pay for the feast.' It was another Zammaramala custom.

El Entierro de la Sardina.

3: Segovian friends

We soon made our first Segovian friends. Alex had put up an advertisement in the local art school offering English classes. At nine o'clock the same evening the doorbell rang. In came Peli, a Segovian painter, who introduced us to his girlfriend Cruz and another friend, Nieves, both of them doctors. Both were beautiful, dark and small, with the kindest of smiles. I had noticed them all in the plaza before but we had still too much of the shy northern temperament in us to make the first move. We sat round the table and offered them wine. They were all in their mid-thirties, a world away from Duque's kitchen.

An elderly Englishman I had bumped into in a nearby village had firm opinions about the3 Spanish and had offered us the wealth of his knowledge. He'd lived in Spain for more than a decade and it was driving him mad. Nothing ever got done. It was the old 'mañana, mañana' cliché. His brief summation of the national character was: 'Insular, inefficient and stupid.' I couldn't see why he'd stayed.

Peli, Cruz and Nieves were quite the opposite. Peli – it was a nickname that alluded to his head of red hair – was a proud Segovian in love with his city and he offered to be my guide. But his wasn't the love of a stay-at-home; it had been born out of nostalgia. He had travelled to every European country, and to most in the Eastern bloc years before they were technically 'open'. On each return to Segovia he admired it more: its architecture, the mountains, the meseta. He and Cruz had shared a year in Peking where she had studied the techniques of acupuncture. One day they would show us the slides. Nieves pulled a piece of chorizo out of her handbag and offered it round. She kept one there for emergencies and as we hadn't stocked up our larder for uninvited guests, now was deemed an emergency. Cruz and Nieves had met as doctors when after leaving Madrid medical school they had been sent to adjoining Segovian hamlets as doctors-in-residence. Nieves joked that the villagers were in her house so often that she had finally had to put a notice above the front door: '*¡No pasarán!*' – the slogan of Republican Madrid that had held out against the Nationalist troops for more than two years – 'They shall not pass'. I laughed and made what I thought was a suitable Spanish exclamation of approval. Peli frowned.

'*Feo, pero muy feo* – very ugly!' My kitchen Spanish had still not got beyond the elemental stage. They asked me what I was doing in Segovia and when I told them they roared with disbelief. I obviously confirmed their opinion about the madness of the English.

'Working in a kitchen? ¡No!' We arranged to meet later at La Concha in the Plaza Mayor for the *último* drink. Our Segovian social life had started in earnest.

Pedro had gone to the doctor's. His back had been hurting him for the previous few weeks. So Mariano had doffed the head chef's high hat. He was firmly in charge. A new chef had started the same day. Felix, a stocky man in his mid-twenties, had moved across to Duque's from one of the lesser known restaurants out in the barrios. Coming to Duque's was a good career move. At first his responsibilities would be less but there was a world of difference between preparing a set meal for ten regular clients and preparing á la carte dishes for up to 300. He had a broad and generous smile, and his enthusiasm proved to be infectious. It only took him a week to join up with his old drinking companion, Santos, and for them to form the kitchen's resident comedy duo.

'Come on, Gisbert. We'll need your help today. Let's start on the red peppers,' ordered Mariano. He was efficient and to the point. Mariano made it clear to the younger chefs that just because Pedro was off there would be no slacking while he was in charge. We were in for a few hard weeks. Next week was carnival and the pinches were bound to burn the midnight oil. They would be asleep on their feet. And after that, during Lent, meant having a full choice of vegetarian dishes on offer. There were still many old people in Segovia who obeyed the strict dietary laws set down by the Church.

One of the delicacies that we could prepare well in advance were preserved red peppers, kept in giant storage crocks. Mariano and I tackled a quantity large enough to keep us going well into the afternoon. The recipe here has been adapted to the needs of a home kitchen for a few weeks' supply. It is the mainstay of any tapas table.

1 kg firm and fleshy red peppers
Head of garlic
Bay leaf and sprig of thyme (optional)
Olive oil
Salt

Dribble a baking tray with olive oil. Lay in the red peppers, sprinkle with salt and put into a medium to hot oven. Alongside lay the peeled garlic cloves. After fifteen minutes look in the oven. If the skin on the top has begun to blister and burn, turn them over. Bake for a further ten to fifteen minutes. Wait until the peppers cool off and start to peel away the skin carefully. A trick is to seal the red peppers in a plastic bag for fifteen minutes and let them steam, and then start. Once the skin is off, carefully seed the peppers, reserving some of the juice that spills out, and cut into bite-size pieces. Lay in the bottom of a sterilized jar, and add a clove of garlic, thyme, and bay-leaf. Fill to close to the top and pour olive oil in until it covers the peppers. Seal and bring out when the appetite calls.

In the best of the Segovian restaurants – Duque's, Cándido's, José María's, Las Columnas, the Parador and Los Arcos – the chef, and possibly the assistant chef, are about the only permanent fixture. The pinches start at sixteen or seventeen. For two years they are the odd-job boys. For another few years they assist the assistants. During this time it is likely that they are called up for military service. If, like Jojo, they have an ambition to carry on in the kitchen, they try to get into the catering corps. None of the chefs come from rich families, so unlike rich kids with *enchufes* – connections – they can't sidestep the obligatory period in the military.

After the period as assistants to the assistants, they might take over responsibility for a particular area in the kitchen. It is a long-drawn-out training and the only way to cut corners is to jump promotion and move on to another restaurant. Most of the assistant chefs choose this route and have worked in various of Segovia's restaurants, in search of promotion, better conditions and better pay. Only a select few rise to the rung of head chef, and only those with an appetite for risk and access to capital can set up on their own.

José María was the exception that proved the rule. He had worked as the sommelier at Cándido's. He was a man in the right place at the right time. The fame of Rioja wines had circled the globe. What few had noticed was the quality of the Ribera de Duero wines, closer to home. José María set up on his own, hired a good chef and offered a table wine of outstanding quality at an extremely cheap price. Segovians flocked to his door. Thus he became an owner.

Santos was preparing himself lunch, a toasted roll of bread with a veal fillet and deep-fried green pepper. He was extremely careful with his food and a keep-fit fanatic, like Mariano. Most afternoons he would get on his racing bike and cover forty to fifty miles. He never drank the red wine-lemonade mix, it was far too fattening. I should have heeded the warning. In one month I put on a stone. My response to the heat of the kitchen was to drink copiously from the carafe. I ate all the meals provided by Pedro, as well as the little tasters prepared from the menu to attune my tastebuds to the subtleties of Castilian cuisine. Now Julián's jacket was tight around the chest.

I went to sit by the open window to cool off in the fresh breeze. The evening before I had had three último gin and tonics, and with Peli, Cruz and Nieves talked late into the night. Each time we were about to leave another friend whom we had to be introduced to walked through the door. It was hopeless saying no and anyway we had to get into training for carnival. At two in the morning, Angulo, a local musician, lifted the piano lid and struck up a tune. The people gathered round and sat the whole way up the stairs of the tiny Negresco bar, joining in with the chorus of 'Tie a Yellow Ribbon round the Old Oak Tree'. The barman pulled down the shutters and locked us in.

'All right then. If you're not getting out, you better have the last one on the house.' From then on we were lost. I sat there quietly, as if in a trance, watching Mariano, Santos and Clemente working hard at the stoves. I pieced the previous night back together again slowly. Every half minute I heard a high-pitched whistle, followed by a group of five notes, from somewhere in the distance, down at the bottom of the hill. I opened the window. There it was again – one note, followed by five.

'Get the knives ready, Clemente. Fernando, you sort out yours and find the poultry shears. Can you see him yet, Gisbert?' See him? See who? 'The knife-sharpener, of course.' I craned my neck out the window and saw an old man pushing his moped slowly up the hill. Santos leant over my shoulder.

'Yes, he's here. I'll go down.' I followed Santos down the stairs and out the back door of the ground-floor bar. It was still too early for the lunchtime crowd and only two or three men stood talking at the bar.

Outside, the knife-sharpener had set up his stall in the street. Santos passed him our box full of knives. We sharpened them on a steel two or three times on a normal working day and now they were ready for a regrind.

A couple of weeks earlier Pedro had given me a class in knife-sharpening. The poultry butcher had walked in and announced pompously that Pedro's method was all wrong. As he was twenty years Pedro's senior, Pedro indulged him. The butcher picked up the knife and steel, and did it in exactly the same way as Pedro, but in reverse.

'So what's the difference between what you're doing and what I did?' asked Pedro.

'Nothing. It's just that I'm left-handed.' He bellowed with laughter.

The knife-sharpener lifted his moped on the stand with the back wheel in the air. On the back rack he had bolted on two different types of grinding stone – one rough, the other smooth. He took out a plastic bottle and asked me to fill it at the bar. He had attached a fanbelt from the back-wheel drive to the coarser of the two stones and set the motor revved up high with an elastic band. It was a primitive system but it worked perfectly. He whistled to himself as he worked, occasionally splashing the stone with water. Santos fetched him wine.

It was not always so friendly with the tradesmen. One day Pedro lost his temper. One of the butchers had come in early one morning and delivered sixty suckling pigs for a large wedding banquet we were preparing. They were in perfect condition, rosy pink and fresh, and we hooked them all up in the cold room, after weighing each one carefully. Pedro wanted to see them. He came out of the cold room steaming, with a piece of offal in his hand. The butcher had inadvertently left a piece of useless innard attached to the cochinillos. Come on, Pedro, I thought to myself, it's not the end of the world. Why get heated up over a matter of pennies? Pedro shouted to Clemente to go down and cut all the little pieces off the sixty cochinillos, and bring them to him. What a waste of time, I thought.

Clemente went down to do it. He had worked with Pedro for years, and knew all his quirks and idiosyncrasies. Half an hour later, Clemente returned. The bag of pieces was weighed: five and a half kilos. At the price in the shop it came to just over 4,000 pesetas; for that amount you could have a good dinner for two in Duque's. Pedro had taught me a valuable lesson.

The knife-sharpener was still honing the blades. Santos told me to wait for them and went back up to work. A few minutes later the man had finished and ambled up the hill playing his pan pipes.

Nieves had asked us over for Sunday lunch. It was the first time we had been invited to someone's house for a meal, discounting Boni and Sagrario's open invitation. The delay wasn't out of an inherent unfriendliness, despite the Segovians' well-known reputation around Spain for being cold and insular. It was just that social life was different here. Gatherings took place in bars and restaurants, before, after, or over a meal.

Nieves's flat was behind the cathedral in the centre of the old Jewish quarter. This is a maze of narrow, winding, cobbled streets lying on the eastern side of the city, above the Clamores river, within the protection of the city walls. At sunset, from the hill opposite, the steep jumble of pitched, tiled roofs glows a deep orange.

Most of the older buildings in the *judería* still have their individual well from which to draw up water. It is always clean and fresh. The supply comes running down directly from the mountains, fed into the city over the Roman aqueduct, an essential life source in this arid, limestone zone.

Segovia's population, over five centuries ago, was roughly the same as it is today, with ninety per cent living within the old city walls. Approximately 20,000 Sephardic Jews crammed themselves into these warren-like houses, with whole families living in a single room. Merchants, cobblers, tailors, financiers to the court, doctors and scientists worked straight from home. It's not surprising that the medieval plagues which decimated Castile hit this area hardest. Nowadays the judería's population is just a tenth of that, and many are weekenders from Madrid, captured and enchanted by the barrio's picturesque charm.

Across the square from Nieves's house a kosher butcher had served up meat to his barrio, without any problems, under the shadow of the

Moorish tower of the Romanesque church of San Andrés. The thirteenth and fourteenth centuries were a golden age of religious tolerance. But unlike Toledo, little remains in Segovia of the Sephardic inheritance, except for the ghost of the synagogue in the Corpus Christi church, and the large round wafers that vendors sell in the Plaza Mayor during fiestas. They could have been *matzos* – paper-thin Jewish wafers.

From Nieves's balcony windows the view was out over the sierra. Across the valley, in the near distance, lay the Jewish burial ground; beyond that, the staggered horizon line of the Guadarrama mountains: the Bola del Mundo – the Ball of the World – Siete Picos – Seven Peaks – and La Mujer Muerte – The Dead Woman. On a clear day eagles, hawks and vultures can be seen circling slowly in the distance looking for rabbits, fieldmice and the odd dead sheep. The most beautiful of all these mountains is La Mujer Muerte. From a distance her outline is easily traceable. She lies there in repose, fingers crossed over her pregnant stomach. As with all Segovian landmarks, La Mujer Muerte comes with her own legend. The real woman was of outstanding beauty, though whether she came from Zammaramala the legend has never made clear.

Her problem was not lack of men but one too many. Two chivalrous suitors, in this land of heroic crusader knights, fought a dramatic duel for the right to her hand. She looked on anxiously. The battle lasted for hours until it reached its inevitable and exhausted conclusion. In the legend, everything now went wrong. Both of the knights were killed, by each other, in their attempt to win her. The mujer walked up the sierra, lay down and died of a broken heart. Which of the two gentleman had got her in the family way was never related.

Nieves was busy in the kitchen preparing lunch. All the other guests were helping too. Peli was slicing up the chorizo. Cruz was laying the table. Vicky and Fernando Esteban, a hilarious medic, were discussing the strength of the cocktail. And Antonio Ruiz, Segovia's official two-tome historian, was decorking a red Rioja.

Nieves was worried. She couldn't possibly cook anything I didn't know how to do better. After two months in Duque's I had put her at a disadvantage. Nonsense. I had still only learnt to make three or four authentic dishes. Our first course was a delicious Segovian offshoot of a well-known Basque speciality; Nieves's *porrusalda* was a poor man's version of a poor man's dish. (The original Basque version also adds salt cod.) It is basically a potato and leek soup, with strong links to

Vichyssoise. Made with plenty of garlic and good olive oil, it is simple but delicious, a quintessential example of all that is best about Castilian cooking: economical, strong in flavour and easy to prepare. Strangers to Castilian food when eating in restaurants often wonder where the vegetables they see in the market have disappeared to. In the home they are almost always served as a starter: stewed as in porrusalda; boiled, drained and then fried with garlic, as in *acelgas con ajo* – a dish of Swiss chard – or *coliflor rebozada* – cauliflower treated in the same way. Then of course there are the simple summer salads, and the cold and refreshing soup, *gazpacho*.

Porrusalda was a favourite dish of Peli's. He was an obsessive and passionate lover of garlic. The garden outside his studio was landscaped on a Chinese model, with giant weeping willows and cherry trees. Small channels of water, fed by a spring, ran through the garden, chuckling and irrigating as they went. At the bottom of the garden, behind box-tree hedge, was a space reserved for garlic-growing that produced enough bulbs to feed a large family for a decade.

'Next week is carnival,' warned Vicky. 'Anyone thought of a costume yet? We'll meet up in Fernando Rey's flat, like last year, and dress up there before the art-school party. You're not going to be too English, are you?'

Pedro was back in the kitchen. He felt fractionally better. Mariano had taken off his toque and replaced it with a small flat cap. They were taking their morning coffee with a sugar bun. For some reason the chicken man had felt we all needed a treat, so he had gone out and bought buns all round. Mariano turned to Fernando and Jojo, and asked them both when they were off to do their military service.

'Sooner the better,' Mariano admonished. 'Look at the pair of them, a complete wash-out.' Fernando had been unlucky. His sixteen-month stretch in the mili was going to start in the late spring, in Melilla, Spain's garrison equivalent to Gibraltar on the North African coast. It would be hot and unpleasant. Jojo was closer to home, in León, and would be able to get back to Segovia on his odd weekend leaves. He had got a place in the catering corps, but he didn't look happy about it. For both, it was to be their first time away from home. 'A year and a half's about enough time to sort you out, Jojo,' said Mariano. Jojo blanched and looked depressed.

'Do you have conscription in England?' he asked, and looked even more pained when I said no. 'Still, I suppose Duque's will have been good training. You ought to see it in here over Easter. It's like the Feeding of the Five Thousand.'

'Today, Gisbert,' announced Pedro, 'I'm going to teach you an easy dish and the next time a client orders it you're going to take over.' He hauled the two concentric rings out of the hot plate with a bent iron hook. He placed an old weathered frying pan straight over the flames and pulled his bottom eyelid down with a finger as a signal for me to watch carefully. Two of the pinches came across for the class. With one hand he broke three eggs into the pan and threw in a handful of wild asparagus tips. He flicked the pan with his wrist, jerking it back and turning the contents. He reached behind him for the salt cellar and from a distance aimed a pinch at the pan that fanned out perfectly as it flew through the air. Another three or four flicks and the mixture was tipped into an earthenware dish. Two triangles of fried bread were stuck in, like ears. It had taken Pedro about thirty seconds. 'There you are, señor. *Revuelto de trigueros*, your breakfast.' I ate it with relish. It was soft and creamy, somewhere between an omelette and scrambled eggs, set off by the crunchy fried bread. It is often eaten as a starter before a fattier dish, like cochinillo or cordero. There are endless varieties of it, the most common being with prawns, wild mushrooms, or artichoke hearts. It is deceptively simple.

Pedro told me to go and stand by the counter where the waiters arrived with their orders.

'Sing them out, Gisbert! And don't forget, as soon as you see the order, over to you.'

It was a good place to stand for kitchen gossip. Each waiter covered a few tables and in their slack periods or waiting for a client's dish to be finished off they would lounge around, sounding off at each other. When it was busy, they would start to trip over one another, so Pedro forced them to stand in a regimental line, queueing out into the hall. They all had nicknames: 'Big Mouth', 'Curly', 'Sourpuss', 'Babyface', 'Punky' and 'Dead Head' – a good kid, said Pedro, but he was pretty short up top. He was doing his parents a favour because they were friends and came from the same barrio. But it didn't look as if he'd got what it takes. He lacked what Pedro called *afición* – a feeling for his work. He was in a permanent dream and fresh out of school. He'd failed his exams, so Pedro was trying to give him a break.

'It's like a crèche in here. I can't believe it sometimes. I ought to go out and buy a dummy to stick in your mouth, Big Mouth, that'll shut you up. Come on, Gisbert, sing out the orders.' I sang. But Santos pretended not to understand. Or, alternatively, Santos just didn't understand. 'Come on Gisbert. Sing. Louder this time. Do an Alfredo Kraus.' I started to sing off the orders: Pedro an entrecôte, Santos two gambas al ajillo, Fernando two plain salad, one mixed, Mariano tortilla with gambas and fillet of veal, Clemente five pigs, two lambs – and make it snappy. They liked my style. Santos was already rushing across with his order completed, with Mariano hard at it behind. The next orders were already coming in. I kept singing. In the organized chaos Santos decided to try one of his jokes. He took a raw fillet steak, and artfully garnished it with slices of tomato and a few leaves of lettuce. When Baby Face moved forward to collect his entrecôte, Santos slipped it on his tray. Baby Face had been working as a waiter for only two weeks. If that was what had been put on his tray, that was what he was taking. He turned round to run up the stairs. Santos panicked.

'Baby Face! Stop! Come back, you half-wit. Baby Face!' He still hadn't twigged, but returned anyway. 'What do you call that?' asked Santos, pointing at the steak.

'Meat?' answered Baby Face meekly. Tears were welling in his eyes. Pedro put his arm round his shoulder.

'Santos is an idiot, but it's a good lesson, just keep an eye on what you're doing. The maître d' has been impressed with your work. Keep it up.' Pedro strolled back to the oven. 'A bloody kindergarten! I just don't know sometimes.'

An order for revuelto de trigueros came in. I ran to the hot plate and Mariano moved over. Three eggs and then the asparagus tips: I broke the eggs, using a knife, one by one into the frying pan. By the time I reached the third the first was already frying. I snatched a handful of asparagus and tossed it on top. Then a generous helping of salt and I tried to flip the mixture. Pedro passed me a spatula to stir it instead. Bits of fried egg stuck to the pan. I scraped them off and poured the mixture into a dish. In went the bread ears and I was ready to pass it to the waiters. I showed it to Pedro but he was not impressed. It's supposed to be moist and mine was dry. Parts of the white had fried to a crust. Pedro, an expression of profound contempt darkening his puckish features, offered it to me.

'Well, Gisbert. Here is your lunch.'

The amount of eggs we got through in the restaurant was phenomenal. They went into all the revueltos and tortillas, and most of the puddings. What they gained by not using butter and cream they made up with eggs. I consulted Pedro's kitchen bible stuck away in his drawer, by the Marqués de Paraberes. In that alone there were 200 egg recipes.

I walked home slowly: I had fallen at the first hurdle. Never mind, I thought, you can't make omelettes without breaking a few eggs.

Concha, the *cartonera*, was walking in front of me. She was about eighty years old, gap-toothed and with a wall eye. Her voice was an eerie crow. She was our barrio's cardboard collector. Every afternoon, when people had retired for siesta, Concha would still be sorting through newspapers and boxes, folding them out to stack flat on her trolley. After a full morning's work she would drag her load off to the depot and get paid for the weight: a few pounds a day. It was a crippling and cruel task in winter but Concha's need was great. Anyway, it was a job like any other and she didn't complain. I doubt if she would have taken charity and she wouldn't be patronized. She winked at me as I went past. She'd put me on her client list. The week before I had sorted out a sack of papers for her and brought them round to the depot by car on my way out to the country. On a good day she would walk into the nearest bar and treat herself to a drink. She was an institution. The shopkeepers shouted as she went by and always kept their best cardboard back for her.

We had given our carnival costumes little thought. By the morning of the art-school party we still hadn't decided. There was no competing with the costumes that had already been seen out on the street: a polar bear, a barman complete with bar, a torero, an upside-down man, and one family who went round as a desk-top computer, a pencil sharpener, a pocket calculator and a fountain pen. There was a toyshop on the calle Réal that sold masks and elaborate costumes but it looked as if most people had spent hours, even days, making their own. The adults made as much effort as the children. Only the over-sixties were exempt.

Patricio, the wild poet of the streets, who looked about seventy, was as game as the rest. He had torn off one of his trouser legs, wrapped his walking stick in crepe paper and tied an apache scarf around his head. He had regaled all the fellow drinkers in Bar Prisco with verse after verse of his own making. Most of it was off-the-cuff improvisation, tailored for the crowd.

When the Bar Prisco clients displayed boredom at Patricio's endless rhyming couplets, he lumbered off down the street declaiming and children followed behind laughing

One day I had encountered Patricio leaning against one of the stone sphinxes that guard the steps of the plaza San Martin. He had a pencil in one hand and was sizeing up the Romanesque church in front of him for a lightning sketch on a piece of crumpled scrap paper. He was deep in concentration. He sang to himself, dreaming in his world of interiors, as he jotted down the view in the most haphazard and sporadic note form.

Suddenly he was startled out of his reverie by two teenagers who had kicked an empty coke can down the steps towards him. His head twisted around violently as he screamed:

'I swear on the mother who once gave birth to me, God rest her soul, that if you do that once again while I'm trying to create a masterpiece, I'll stick a letterbomb down the front of your trousers and blow your eggs off – both pairs!' He made a lunge towards the boys but they stood their ground. Everyone knew Patricio, a harmless man whose bark was worse than his bite.

His only sin, if it could so be called, was the sin of imagination. He brooded heavily on man's destiny. He stopped me in the street outside Bar Columnas on a rainy afternoon and invited me in for a drink. I could join him on condition that he would pay, otherwise I might as well forget it.

I wasn't a Segovian he knew well. And that was precisely the reason he wanted to speak to me. With deadly seriousness he opened the discussion. His lively eyes fixed on me without blinking.

'Is there an afterlife? Is there?'

Embarrassed by the directness of his question I tried to fob him off with something non-committal. But it didn't satisfy him. This wasn't the moment for philosophical meanderings. He needed and demanded an answer. And it was something I couldn't supply. We left the bar together 'in peace', as he put it, but I had disappointed him.

The Trades and Crafts College walked past the balcony, the full complement of 101 Dalmatians. What could we make in only three hours? I thought I'd left behind the world of fancy dress sixteen years before, and we weren't old enough yet for vicars and tarts. Dominoes! An inspired idea! At least we wouldn't lose total face. We blacked up, slipped on our cardboard numbers, and went round to show Boni and Sagrario. They were indulgent.

'Not bad.' Sagrario was particularly excited by Alejandra.

We walked up to Fernando's flat avoiding Duque's door. I was certainly not going to let the boys on the evening shift see me. Everyone and his dogs were out, and even one of those had been dressed up with ribbons and bows. We walked down past the church of San Estéban and entered Fernando Rey's courtyard where the salsa was deafening. Up in the flat all of our new friends were gathered. The women had raided their wardrobes and emptied out their make-up kits. Stockings, Hawaiian shirts, bin-liners, cardboard, staple-guns, sellotape, silver foil, wrapping paper and crash helmets lay littered across the floor. Carmen's costume of a Cockney queen was already finished, but she was more embarrassed at her efforts than we were at ours. Cruz went sophisticated Chinese.

The tiny bathroom was packed to bursting. Pilar sat on the loo while Vicky made up her face. She was going to be the fairy on top of a Christmas tree. Fernando was crammed in the corner craning to see the mirror with a stocking pulled over his head. He had overdone it on the make-up and was wiping his first efforts off. Out in the living room the table was strewn with bottles of spirits and wine, and the sad leftovers of an even sadder tapas table. The consumption of food was of secondary importance.

'Get a glass out of the kitchen and help yourself,' suggested Fernando, dressed up as Wyatt Earp. Tonight was no night for moderation. We had to go the whole hog. The atmosphere was zany and frivolous. The others had been there for an hour or so and we had a good deal of catching up to do. The first treble whisky went straight down the hatch.

In the furthest room, Diego was wrestling with his creation. He had stolen his son's plastic Viking helmet and was transforming himself into a fighting bull. His tights were tight enough but what looked the most painful was the lump on his back. Peli was becoming a wood spirit and needed help attaching the ivy. Another round of whiskies was poured. Caché made his impressive stage entrance as an upmarket Count Dracula, blood capsules and all. Camped-up screams of horror drowned the salsa. We were ready to go.

The Plaza Mayor was a scene of total pandemonium. Cartoon figures, caricatures, all sorts of creatures and creations forced their way into already full bars. Orders were shouted over the tops of heads. In Bar Negresco, Soto looked me over sceptically and asked why I had bothered. With a nose like mine, he said, all I needed to do was put an elastic band around my ears and pretend.

A small minority of the older generation had come out in their everyday clothes to watch, but their sobriety had no effect on the general hilarity. Drunken backslapping and expressions of surprise were about the only forms of communication that could cut through the full-blown assault on the senses. Half the fun was guessing who was behind the disguise. It was a nightmare for the waiters – a lot of unpaid bills were left behind. At the door of the art school the queue went down the hill. It was full already but we all got in. The noise was deafening and the heat incredible. In one corner a drunken leopard had passed out. It was the last image of the night that remained firmly in my mind.

We had given carnival a good run. We hadn't stayed up as late as many of our friends every night, but four in the morning didn't seem excessively early to me. How did they do it? Some of them were doctors and would be on duty by eight. We had joined in and at least made a feeble attempt to construct our carnival costumes.

Hungover and bleary eyed, I found Ash Wednesday morning a relief. Excess had shocked the system. The first few minutes after waking up I planned a strict programme of spiritual and physical purging. I would try to obey the dietary laws of a Catholic lent and as a symbol of my willingness I had decided to visit the cathedral during mass. In the afternoon I would go to Duque's and work the second shift – lunch was bound to be quiet.

Out in the street there was no one between the age of eight and eighty. The sun was out but it was freezing cold and dangerously slippery on the cobbles where some of the shop-keepers had thrown out their water. I decided to take the long way round to avoid passing Duque's. Santos's sense of humour was not something I felt like facing at this early hour. Anyway, I thought, I didn't want to create any ill feeling by giving them the impression I was some kind of *señorito* who could turn up when he liked – which was how it was, of course.

I rounded the corner into the plaza San Estéban and saw the most extraordinary sight. On the only area of the square that had come into sunlight was a man with his back to me kneeling on a double, king-size mattress. He was huddled over forwards and his right arm was shooting backwards and forwards rhythmically. I moved closer to him, hoping I wasn't being indiscreet. He didn't stop at the sound of my footsteps but just carried on regardless, forwards, backwards, forwards, backwards. In his right hand he held a curved carpet needle and was patiently stitching up the side of the mattress. I asked him what he was doing.

'Nothing much. Just turning the mattress for the woman up there, Blanca. You know her, don't you? Her husband's got the ferretería on calle Réal.' I looked up to the top balcony and there was Blanca leaning over to make sure her mattress was being turned over properly. I'd never seen her before. 'You're not from Segovia, are you? I can tell by your accent.' I took it as a compliment.

It was spring-cleaning time and the mattress man went from barrio to barrio as a journeyman, beating out, respreading and refilling the uncomfortable old horsehair mattresses. All Blanca's windows were wide open, despite the cold, airing the flat and chasing out the stale odours of winter.

The mass was a solemn and funereal occasion. It was the crossover point into Lent; all our previous indulgences, culminating in the orgiastic excesses of carnival, were to be replaced with a healthy period of abstinence. The congregation, however, almost all octogenarian women, didn't look as if they were the sinning sort. I hadn't seen many of them at the art-school party the night before. For them the noise and disturbances of carnival were a relatively recent thing, or remembered way back from their youth, before the Civil War. During Franco's dictatorship carnival had been banned.

The most important part of the mass had arrived. The congregation filed forward towards the waiting bishop. With the ashes of the burnt palms he marked the women with a cross on their forehead and the men on their crown. With these marks he repeated to every penitent:

'You are now as ash and you will end as ash – ashes to ashes, dust to dust.' It was strangely moving and I felt somehow refreshed by the austerity of the service.

It wouldn't last for long. Next day, in the kitchens, I would have to face the practical jokes and horsing around of Pototo, Santos and Clemente, though with a clearer idea of the life of their city. What strange things I had seen over the last few days: the most surreal costumes imaginable, normally retiring sorts transformed into roaring drunken lions, a mattress man, and then the sobering mass. None of it compared with what I met down by the aqueduct on my way home.

As I rounded the corner into the calle San Francisco I ran into a group of thirty or forty women, mourners of all ages, from young girls to grandmothers. They were dressed from head to toe in black, crowned with elegant mantillas in their hair, their faces covered by finely worked lace veils. The procession took up the full width of the street and I had to step back in the doorway of the butcher's to let them pass. They shuffled forward in various states of grief. Their white silk handkerchiefs dabbed at self-induced tears, and these gestures were accompanied by strangled whimpers and heart-rending sobs. In the centre of the group, high up on their shoulders, transported like a coffin, was a six-foot-long sardine, constructed out of papier mâché. It was exactly the same scene that Goya had painted almost two centuries before: *El Entierro de la Sardina* – The Funeral of the Sardine.

The procession was a hybrid of the pagan and anti-clerical demonstrations of the previous century, and the conservative attitudes of the organized church. It was difficult to know whether the celebrants were drawing attention to the end of carnival or the beginning of Lent; the event couldn't seem to make its mind up.

I let the procession pass and followed on behind. The mourners became increasingly dramatic and intense in their expressions of grief. The older women in particular appeared genuinely affected by the role that they had chosen to play. Their mourning was uninhibited; they had acted themselves into the part, with faces twisting and contorting into masks of pity and pain. The youngest girls were more self-conscious, vainer perhaps. Their friends were watching, and they were still too young for the necessary qualities of sincerity and gravitas to have developed to the full. They couldn't decide whether to laugh or cry.

Throughout, the giant sardine rolled about clumsily on their shoulders, from side to side, oblivious to the attentions and the displays of emotion below. Inching its way forward to its final resting site, this decidedly landlocked fish hadn't the slightest idea it was on the way to its funeral. At last the procession reached the aqueduct. Under the central arch the sardine was gently lowered and laid down on a bed of kindling. It was the perfect place to perform the rite. High above in a niche sat the Virgin Mary decorated with a sash of Spain's national colours. Centuries before, Hercules had stood there, the aqueduct presumably one of his unrecognized labours. The pagan statue had been replaced by the Christian Virgin some time after the Reconquista.

The women formed a circle round the sardine and one of them put a torch to the pyre. The papier mâché fish disappeared in a flash. The flames leapt up, the women drew away from the intense heat and the crowd slowly dispersed – a heap of ashes left smouldering amongst the cobbles.

What did it mean? Why on the first day of Lent burn a fish, the very foodstuff that isn't proscribed? It didn't make sense. I asked our historian friend.

More than two hundred years ago, before Madrid was linked to any other city or fishing port by rail and produce was transported by mule, it would take weeks for the fish to arrive. The staple diet in those days was salt cod, salted herrings, anchovies and sardines – anything that stood a chance of remaining in an edible state over the long journeys through central Spain. On one particular Ash Wednesday, the devout population of Madrid was waiting on the banks of the Manzanares river for the precious mule train to arrive. Finally, a voice in the crowd called out, 'It's here! It's arrived at last!' and the crowd surged forward to meet it. The fish, however, had been badly packed and salted, and had started to ferment in the barrels. By the time they got the sardines out of the barrels they were a festering, putrid soup. The whole delivery was burnt on the spot. From its beginnings in Madrid, the Funeral of the Sardine passed into Castilian folklore and is now celebrated everywhere.

By two o'clock I was back in the restaurant alongside Pedro.

'It's a joke. Look at the shambles. Pototo can hardly open his eyes, Jojo's asleep and Felix is up in the clouds. I suppose you were out last night as well, Gisbert. It's like a fairground in here. I should have bought you all lollipops to suck on. Right. We've got two parties of forty to cook for and they're due in ten minutes. There's some lunch left over for you, Gisbert, there in the pot. I thought you had gone on summer holidays.'

I looked over at Pototo and he smiled back conspiratorially. His eyes were bloodshot, narrow slits. I had left him in the small plaza Santa Eulália dancing to the band at four in the morning and from there he said he was going on to the Plaza Mayor. I mouthed across to him, 'Tired?' and he gestured back with a certain pride, 'No. Not at all.'

'Are you going to have any lunch or not, Gisbert? Because otherwise I'm taking it off the stove.'

'Yes, what is it?'

'*Patatas a la importancia*, our token start to Lent.'

It smelt wonderful, the perfect plain filler for after a long night out. Slices of potato were gently boiled in their eggy envelopes and flavoured with a wine and saffron sauce. The contrast in texture was a bit strange, the soft elastic egg set off by the crumbly potato, but for something so simple it was an ingenious dish. It wasn't on the restaurant menu because it was plain home cooking, and nobody comes out to eat what they can have at home.

I asked Pedro if people were still reasonably strict about Lent. Mariano exploded into laughter.

'You watch on Friday. We'll prepare a special fish dish and a vegetarian pâté, and look at what they order: chorizo to start with and cochinillo to follow.'

Pedro told me that Lent had never really been a time of sacrifice, not in the city. It may have been different in the outlying superstitious villages. Anyway, in the Hunger Years it had been like ten never-ending years of Lent for many. Friday is the only day that some people still bother to observe, and usually just the old. Even then there's a way of getting round the restrictions without losing face.

Pedro explained. On Friday morning you wake up exhausted. All night long, because you know that you're not allowed to have one, you dream of a giant tender solomillo steak surrounded by a few of the spicy green peppers from the village of Padrón. You're sweating with greed and not a little guilt. What do you do? Easy. You go to confession and talk to the priest. You bow your head in shame for the sin you are about to commit, and say:

'Father. I beg God's forgiveness. It is Lent and on top of that it's a Friday. In about approximately four hours twenty minutes, after I've had a first course of asparagus with a generous helping of mayonnaise – good Lenten fare, don't you agree, Father?'

'Yes, my son, speak up. What is your sin?'

'Well... I will consume a solomillo with spicy green peppers and covered in a thin layer of jamón serrano.'

The sinner buys his bula from the priest, a fine that bears some relation to the ten per cent service charge added to the bill in London restaurants, and is automatically forgiven his forthcoming sin.

For those who are more conscientious about Lent or whose store cupboard has run down to potatoes, a few eggs and the dregs of last night's bottle of white wine, this is Pedro's excellent version of *patatas a la importancia.*

1 kg potatoes	*1 tbsp chopped parsley*
2 to 3 eggs (whisked)	*Pinch of saffron*
Flour	*1 glass dry white wine*
2 tbsp olive oil	*1 glass chicken stock*
1 onion, finely diced	*Water*
2 cloves garlic	*1 bay leaf*

Salt to taste

Peel the potatoes. Cut into slices as thick as your little finger. Wash, drain and dry. Dredge the potatoes in flour, followed by the egg, and deep fry for a few minutes. In a large casserole fry the onions, the finely diced cloves of garlic and bay-leaf in the olive oil until pale gold. On top of this carefully lay out the potatoes in layers. Add the stock, wine, saffron and parsley, and as much water as is needed to cover the potatoes. Simmer gently for twenty minutes and serve. The dish is sometimes finished off with a sprinkling of boiled egg chopped finely, diced tomato and olives stuffed with anchovies.

In Segovia the resulting sauce is sometimes poured on the leftover slices of the day's tortilla and served up as a tapa before the following day's lunch.

4: An Orchestra Pit

Life in the flat became like being in an orchestra pit. It started with the dawn reveille, across the street, from over the walls of the military academy. Conscripts were learning the cornet. The same few notes were repeated over and over again. Occasionally, a novice would break into an improvised solo. The sound was terrible.

In the afternoon the noise was concentrated round the back of the flat. Someone was practising the *dulzaina* – a sawn-off Segovian clarinet, which sounded like the bagpipes – in his garage. The only one entertained by this performance was Electric Martín's alsatian, shut up in the courtyard below. He howled in accompaniment. Electric was our downstairs neighbour and at nights his mangy beast would sit in the button shop, keeping guard against imaginary assailants. Then, at eight o'clock in the evening, the boys' brigade would take over in the square down the hill. Twenty teenage drummers stood in a circle under the yellow streetlights, beating out their tribal rhythms.

One morning we woke up and sensed there was something wrong. There was a deathly silence. Was there another fiesta that Pedro had forgotten to warn me about? I opened the wooden shutters. On the roof opposite a few feet of snow had appeared overnight. It was still falling fast and settling on the street. It looked like we were in for a white Easter.

I asked the butcher below us if this was abnormal.

'Abnormal? No. We've had blizzards here in June. It doesn't settle though, it'll all be gone by the late afternoon. Years ago, when I was a young man, it used to be much colder. We would have snow on the streets for weeks. Something funny is happening with the weather.'

I walked through the snow to Duque's.

'Do you want to come skiing with me this afternoon?' asked Mariano. 'It's perfect powder snow up on the Bola del Mundo. Today's going to be quiet, anyway, two of the passes across the mountains to Madrid have been closed off. I might even sleep up there on the mountain tonight. By the way, have you got chains for your car?'

I dried my shoes out next to the oven. The snow was already turning to slush. It was warm in the kitchen but damp and it felt as if I was breathing water. I wondered what Pedro would prepare para familia today. The roasting would be difficult, for a start; it always was with a change of the weather. Clemente had opened his end of the range up and was driving in air with an electric fan. It was ten o'clock and we still hadn't put in any coal. There was almost no draw on the chimney. Fernando had started the fire up at eight, but outside it was wind-still and now it would take twice as long to bring the oven up to temperature.

I looked around for my oven cloths. They had all disappeared.

'Ask Dominga,' said Santos, 'she's out in the hall.' I didn't know the Spanish word for 'oven cloth', so I asked Santos. 'Bragas,' he said. Dominga was down on her hands and knees scrubbing the floor.

The washer-upper women, despite their weekly English classes were still standoffish and wary. We didn't mix much. There was some half-hearted flirtation but most of the time they lived in their world and we in ours. I asked her politely for my 'bragas'. She screamed with laughter. Santos skulked his corner. What was up now? Dominga was choking and called to Rellés.

'"Give me your knickers," he said. That boy is too naughty for words.'

Dominga was a handsome woman, strong featured, with short fairish hair. She was in her late thirties, and reminded me of an aunt of mine. She had lived in Karlsrühe for four years where her husband had worked as a Gastarbeiter in the Mercedes factory. It was a good job and the pay was higher than he would get in Spain. I tried to imagine a Mediterranean getting used to northern ways of life, but it was impossible. With no life on the street, stuck there in Karlsrühe in an industrial desert after the beauty of Segovia and the grandeur of the meseta, it must have been terrible for her. She had suffered from chronic homesickness and so had her husband. German was an impossible language to learn. Where were the fiestas? The siestas? And the family meals? They hadn't lived a day without dreaming of home. But that was the one thing that the four years in Germany had bought them: a home.

'Another six months here at Duque's and we'll have saved enough to get our own bar,' she enthused.

'Do you enjoy your job here?' I asked her. She looked at me as if I was a half-wit. She said nothing and didn't need to. Two hours on your hands and knees, scrubbing four floors of a restaurant, hardly goes down as one of the world's great pleasures. She stood up and stuck her mobcap on my head.

'Go and show Santos.' The tears rolled down her cheeks.

'What's going on down there?' shouted Duque.

'Nothing,' said Pedro, as he stepped grinning into the hall. 'Come on, Gisbert. Here's your cloth. Today, I'll show you a Lenten special. *Potaje*. It's very good.' One of the delivery men, an ugly Velázquez drunkard, had brought in a beautiful box of spinach.

½ kg chickpeas
250 g bacalao (salt cod, a cheaper cut: the bony tail end)
250 g spinach
250 g potatoes
1 boiled egg
2 tbsp olive oil
1 slice white bread
2 cloves garlic
Pinch of saffron
Salt to taste

Chop up the bacalao and put to soak the night before along with the chickpeas. Boil the chickpeas until tender (speed up the process with a pressure cooker). Drain and put in a pan large enough to hold all of the ingredients. Clean the bacalao, removing skin and bones, without reducing to a flaky paste. Boil the spinach for two minutes. Drain. Squeeze out excess water and chop up roughly. Fry the sliced garlic and bread in olive oil till both are golden. Crush up finely in a pestle and mortar. In the same oil fry the spinach until it absorbs the oil. Throw in with the chickpeas. Add the bacalao, and the peeled and quartered potatoes. Add a pinch of saffron to the pestle and mortar, and a large glass of water. Mix and add to the pan, with extra water to cover the potatoes. Boil until tender. Taste and season with salt. Just before serving, chop up the egg yolk finely and stir into the potaje. Put it out on a serving dish and sprinkle with the chopped egg white.

This is Pedro's version, but there are other local variations and many more across Spain. One of Spain's earliest cooks, Juan Altamiras, a Franciscan priest, noted down the recipes prepared in his monastery in Aragón. His recipe exchanged white beans for the chickpeas. Father Bartolomé, a Barefoot Carmelite from Úbeda, avoided the use of bacalao.

Potaje is typically Castilian, argued Pedro. Until there was a decent public transport set up, from coast to capital, the supply of fresh fish would remain sporadic. One fish, the sea bream, earned its nickname, the 'mule killer', for obvious reasons. But in modern terms it wouldn't be regarded as fresh at all. Bacalao, and salted anchovies and herrings, were about the only ones that could be expected not to perish. They repaid the effort and cost of the transport. It wasn't surprising, then, continued Pedro, that in the area of Spain furthest from the sea bacalao was often used.

It was the Basques, Castile's northern neighbours, who as the first major whaling nation discovered an unlimited supply of cod off the coast of Newfoundland. Gutted and strung up in the salty winds on the return trip across the Atlantic, the bacalao arrived back in Europe as a solid plank of protein. In Segovia, the best place to buy bacalao is not in the fishmonger's, but in the *ultramarinos*. It is no longer the cheap staple it used to be, but it is still affordable. In a dish like potaje, its savoury strength stretches a long way.

My favourite ultramarinos – which literally means 'from over the seas' – was down at the bottom of our street, opposite Cándido's. It was an Aladdin's cave, stocked floor to ceiling with temptation: five different types of ham, including the rare acorn-fed ham from the wild Iberian pig, every type of bean, chickpea and lentil, chorizo, morcilla and another ten types of cured meat. Then came all the tinned specialities, plastic containers of top-quality saffron, olive oils and herbal infusions. Every single purchase, however small, was wrapped with the care we normally reserve for Christmas presents. There was nothing more pleasurable than to spend a few minutes window shopping on my way home from Duque's, or later, when it had opened, to idle away a quarter of an hour browsing through the shelves.

A permanent fixture on the end of the counter of any half-decent ultramarinos is the bacalao guillotine. It often takes a frustrating length of time and aptitude for delicate – or bloody-minded – negotiation but eventually you get any cut of the fish you want. The central fillet is for eating raw, after soaking, with a salad of oranges, the outer edges for a potaje and the bony tail for soup. The more expensive boneless scraps need no more than an hour's soak, but I enjoy the ritual and the sense of anticipation. To see and handle the next day's lunch four or five times before the final preparation is a sure way of whetting the tastebuds.

News of the English classes was spreading fast by word of mouth. The latest pupil was a Frenchwoman. She had come to Segovia as a student to write a thesis on the Fiesta of St Agatha of Zammaramala, had fallen in love, married and stayed. Cata was choosy about where she shopped. The *quesería* in the Jewish quarter was where she bought her cheese. Her fillet steak and ham came from a butcher half an hour's walk away. And her vegetables and eggs came direct from the nuns. We had seen one of the chicken farms on a trip out to the country and as a consequence had spent the last few weeks looking for free-range eggs. Cata offered to introduce me to the nuns. Couldn't she tell me where it was to save her the trouble of taking me? Of course, she said, but it wasn't a shop with normal opening and closing hours. It was better if she came.

A few days later we went together to see the nuns of San Vicente. The convent was outside the city walls, so we drove down by car. Across from the barrio of San Lorenzo we could see the walled gardens of the convent with its beehives. A good thaw had set in and for the first time in the year it was actually warm enough to take off your jumper. We parked the car and walked in through the convent gate.

'Did you bring an egg box? No. Well, maybe Sister Angeles will have a spare.'

The nuns of San Vicente are members of a closed order. Judging by the size of the building, there could have been hundreds of them devoting themselves to prayer. Now there are only eight and only one under the age of sixty. The only people ever allowed into the building are the odd electrician repair man and, of course, a doctor.

Cata and I stepped into a plain white waiting room. There was no decoration save for some obscene graffiti that someone had carved into the plasterwork in English, but they had got the spelling wrong. Set into one of the walls was a large wooden shutter held closed by a chain that disappeared through a hole in the wall. Cata rang the bell; in the far distance we could hear it echoing through the building. We waited for a few minutes, and then the chain started to rattle and the shutter opened.

Inside was a large wooden turnstile with two layers of shelves. It had been set into the wall carefully so that when it turned it was never possible to see inside the building. It was the nuns' only form of communication with the outside world. All their supplies entered the convent through this turnstile; there were still crumbs from the baker's early delivery lying on the shelf. From the other side of the turn-stile we heard a solemn, faltering voice.

'Ave María Purísima.'

And Cata replied, 'Sin pecada concebida' (conceived without sin). If I came on my own in the future I would have to respect this formality.

'Hi, Cata. How are you today?' said the invisible voice.

'Very well, Sister Angeles. It looks as if spring is on its way, at last. What a winter we've had, sister. It's been very hard. Did you keep warm enough yourselves?'

'Yes, yes, by the grace of God. But it's the first time we 've been able to go out and work in the garden, properly, for any length of time. We're a bit behind this year. The children aren't with you today, Cata?'

'No, Sister Angeles. Miguel's gone up to the stables with Luis to feed the horses and Elena's playing with a friend. I've brought an English friend along to meet you.' I greeted her in a formal and respectful way.

'Enchanted to meet you,' she said. 'Have you been living in Segovia long? It's a very beautiful city.'

It must be a strange existence. From within their garden walls they can look out across the valley to the mediaeval city walls. They can see the towers of San Estéban church, San Andrés and San Nicolás. The only indication of progress and change they can possibly see are the giant orange cranes hovering threateningly over the Plaza Mayor. Some time later in the year the cranes would be dismantled and it would be as if nothing had happened. Their view of the city hasn't changed in a lifetime. It must be like looking at a picture postcard all day long. Their bird's-eye view of the city is suspended in space and time.

'Well, Cata, what can I do for you today? Jai, the owner of La Concepción, was down here earlier to collect some of our first flowers of the year and some spinach for his chef.' When setting up his bar, Jai had kept the name of the previous tenants – a religious outfitters and ecclesiastical bookshop. He was a big supporter of the convent's produce.

'Sister Angeles, you don't have a spare egg box for my English friend? He forgot to bring one.'

'Yes, I think so, but will you bring it back?' Necessity was obviously the legitimate mother of ecology.

'Can we have two dozen eggs? And a kilo of spinach? Is there any of last year's honey left?'

Cata put her empty egg box in the turnstile. It disappeared with a loud creaking noise as the heavy oak turnstile was moved round slowly by Sister Angeles from inside.

'Be patient, Cata. It might take a few minutes to pick the spinach.' We heard the shuffle of feet and then all was silent. I turned round to Cata and whispered. They couldn't possibly make a living out of these small daily sales. And what about the winter when they had nothing to sell? No, she explained, this was just their pocket money, a little extra on the side. Their real bread and butter came from painting the hot and cold symbols onto the heads of bathroom taps. It must be crucifyingly boring but at least it left them time to spare for their devotions.

'Here we are, Cata. There's all that you asked for. But I'm afraid there's no honey left. There's just enough left over for ourselves. I'm sorry.' The turnstile came creaking back round. The spinach was laid out on a beautiful hand-woven straw dish, a simple and elegant still life. Cata put the spinach in her bag and left the basket on the turnstile. 'Two dozen eggs at 160 pesetas each.' Sister Angeles was doing her calculations out loud. 'We take the 60 from the second dozen and add it to the 160 of the first. That's 220. Add the 100 left over from the second dozen to the 220 from the first dozen which includes the 60 from the second dozen. That's 320. The spinach is 70 a kilo. That means if I add the 70 of the spinach to the 320 of the two dozen eggs... No, hang on, that's not right. Yes it is. The total comes to 390.

The one dozen eggs is for your English friend, so that's 160, and yours, Cata, is 160 plus seventy, which comes to...'

'We'll pay for this together,' Cata jumped in quickly.

'If you've got 400 pesetas, that will be easier. Then I can give you two duros change.' (*Duro*, meaning 'hard one', is the old colloquial description of the five-peseta piece, still used sometimes in the vegetable market and bars.) Cata put in her money and around came the change.

'Thank you, Sister Angeles, and stay in good health.'

'Goodbye, Cata, and may God go with you. Give a big kiss to Miguel and Elena for me, and tell them to come and see me soon. It was very nice to meet your English friend. Remember to bring back the cardboard box, won't you? See you both soon.' The chain rattled and the wooden shutter closed. Leaving the room I noticed a small hand-written notice announcing their opening times during Easter.

'I haven't taught you to make a single pudding yet, have I, Gisbert? A meal without a pudding is like a beautiful woman with only one eye,' said Pedro.

The sweet trolley in a typically Castilian restaurant is not its strongest suit. In most restaurants I would choose the mature Manchego cheese, made from 100 per cent ewe's milk, which always comes in a thick slice, accompanied by a knife and fork. It is usually more than enough for two people. Curiously enough, taking into account the Castilians' love for bread with everything they eat, neither bread nor biscuits are ever served with the cheese. Since the first meal in our flat, when we had forgotten to supply bread, our friend Vicky would always telephone before coming round to see if we wanted her to pick some up on the way. In restaurants I always have to ask for a little bread to be brought with the cheese and sometimes I receive a puzzled look, as if I were breaking some terrible taboo. The one time that no bread is required with the cheese is when it is served with a slice of sweet quince jelly – membrillo. This jelly is particularly good with the sharp Manchego cheeses that have matured for months in a bath of olive oil.

The sweet that Pedro was going to teach me was a cheap, bread-based dessert, called *torrijas*, that appears everywhere for the forty days of Lent. It can be eaten at any time of day: for breakfast, as a pudding after lunch, with tea, after supper, or in the Plaza Mayor late at night in a bar with hot chocolate. The old Segovian ladies are particularly keen on torrijas as they are known to have medicinal properties. With the change from a dry winter to a damp spring, they are supposed to ward off a cold. Quite naturally, a cold was something they were frightened of and you would often see them walking up the street with a handkerchief clamped tightly over mouth and nose. It wasn't against the smog and pollution, because in Segovia there is none, but to stop freezing cold air entering directly into their lungs.

Like sopa castellana, a good torrijas is made with old stale bread, the leftovers from the day before. The recipe works better using it – the texture and resistance are exactly right. In the Castilian peasant kitchen almost nothing is thrown away. Wastefulness is regarded as a decadent sin. In one bar out in one of the tiny sierra villages, they have made the fly curtains at the entrance door out of thousands of overlapping squashed beer-bottle tops. Time is not important but resources are.

3 eggs	*4 slices white peasant bread*
½ litre milk	*4 tbsp olive oil*
150 g caster sugar	*Ground cinnamon to taste*

2 tbsp honey (optional)

Beat up 100 g of caster sugar with the milk. Dip a slice of bread into the milk until it is good and wet. Dip this into the beaten egg and fry in the oil until it becomes light brown on both sides. Repeat. Put this on a serving dish, sprinkle with the caster sugar and cinnamon, and pour over the leftover milk. Dribble with honey and put into the fridge for two or three hours. To make the torrijas 'drunk', pour over a glass of Moscatel, Málaga or sweet sherry.

In the olive and pickle shop on our shopping street, the owner had recently changed his display. Out went the dried chestnuts and in went a windowful of garlic. From floor to ceiling, garlic ruled, filling four square metres. They were ready for their April planting. After every English class Peli would pass by the shop and admire them. Along calle Réal the clothes shops were also in the process of changing all their window displays. Spring is the time for weddings. For children, it is the moment for their first communion. The best day to celebrate it is on Palm Sunday.

Just as I was leaving the restaurant to go home Pedro asked me if I would work on Palm Sunday. I hadn't really seen the kitchen working at full capacity yet and it would be good experience – a chance also, I thought, to display a bit of solidarity with the other chefs. Since I had arrived at Duque's I couldn't help but be singled out as a special case, and I sensed, more from the waiters than the chefs, a little resentment. One of the older waiters had on occasion been particularly sour, as if to say, What the hell are you doing here anyway? It was their life, a hard sacrifice of long and anti-social hours. How could I ever understand what it was really like for them? I could always get up and leave when I wanted, and they knew it. My novelty value had worn off and the honeymoon was over. Of course I would work on Palm Sunday, I told Pedro, but only if he thought I would be useful and I wouldn't get in the way.

'Gisbert, you're part of the furniture now. No one can sing out the orders quite like you.' In the worst analysis I could serve as light entertainment on a hot and sweaty day. Last year on Palm Sunday they had had a record intake. On top of all the communion lunches, crowds of madrileños had flooded up to Segovia on the first good sunny weekend of the year.

That afternoon I drove out to the palace at Riofrio, four miles west of Segovia. It had been built as the hunting palace for the Bourbon kings and was surrounded by parkland in which deer roamed free. Just up from the palace a small chorizo factory had set itself up, and was specializing in wild-boar and venison chorizo from animals culled on the estate. They were eaten more out of curiosity than for any other reason; they were expensive and only half as good as those made from the meat of the humble pig.

Hunting, in the past, had provided an important supplement to the Segovian diet, but the Socialist government, advised by ecologists and animal behaviourists, had been reducing the days on which you could shoot, year after year. An increasing number of animals had come under official protection. It was a good thing but it angered the farmers greatly. Now more than ever it has become a sport for gentlemen, rich Americans and Europeans, who can shoot almost whenever they want on the large private estates of the aristocracy.

Mushrooms, wild herbs and bitter salad greens, on the other hand, were free, for anyone. A few days earlier a toothless and weathered mushroom picker had come into the restaurant with a gigantic sack of morels (tooth extraction being the only dental treatment you can get free on the health service). I asked him where he had picked them but even with Pedro's intervention, or possibly because of it, we could get no more accurate description than 'up in the hills above Segovia'. It was how he made his living. Whenever wild foods of any description came into season he would be out collecting them: mushrooms, herbs for infusions, golden thistle stalks, chestnuts and blackberries. I decided to go out and try for mushrooms myself. After two hours of tracking backwards and forwards below the shade of the oak trees I was 100 per cent unsuccessful. It didn't matter, as I was enjoying the walk. After three months in the restaurant it was exercise I needed the most.

I walked on slowly inhaling the fresh air for another hour and followed a fast-flowing mountain brook that had broken its banks and flooded a meadow. Bent over in the sun were two old women filling their baskets with greenery. What was it? I asked.

'*Perifollo*. It's a Segovian speciality. It's the only place in Spain you can find it. You can't beat it for taste, but it has a very short season in the spring. We're collecting it for José María. Try some.' It grows in the mountain brooks and meadows fed by the melting snow waters of the sierra; it is delicious, with a strong taste of iron. It is miniature water-cress and the collecting of it is labour-intensive. You can't pick it, because too much earth comes up with the root, so instead you crop it with scissors, as if cutting someone's hair. The only precaution you need to take is to wash it in a large bucket of water along with a teaspoon of bleach. After an hour any bugs sink to the bottom and you then wash it well again under a running tap of cold water. It's a fine delicacy and dressed only with vinegar, olive oil and salt it cuts the fat off even the heartiest Segovian winter meal. So, did this mean it was spring? I asked the women. 'Heavens, no. We don't have spring in Segovia, we go straight from winter into summer.' When, then, did winter end here? It couldn't be far off. 'It depends on the weather! Some years are worse than others but we have a golden rule. On 24 June we put our fur coats away. I've never seen frost after that, apart from two years ago, but that was an exception.'

Another two months, I thought. The idea filled me with desperation. I could take the cold, but not the heating bills. Perhaps Sagrario and Boni's heater, under the dining-room table, was the only way of getting through a Segovian winter without taking out a bank loan. It was an old-fashioned sort that used very little electricity. But our flat was light and spacious, and I couldn't limit my life to one tiny area of it. I hoped that the alarmist old sages were wrong.

On Palm Sunday I was told by Pedro to be in early: not only had the range been lit but also the gigantic bread oven in the basement that could roast forty cochinillos at a time – Jojo had started it the night before, gradually building up the temperature. It was already at 350°C. Through the trapdoor, I could see the flames blasting through. Every half hour Jojo slipped out of the kitchen and fed the fire with more vine cuttings until finally he raked it out. Today would be different, warned Pedro, you'll sleep well tonight. Many clients would forget about their normal lunch and come in at 1pm. We would have to speed everything up. Pedro put me in charge of the tapas preparation. It would free the pinches for other more pressing tasks.

Mariano, normally very friendly, had no time for niceties today. He was moving round the kitchen at a sprint. Pedro spent an hour barking out orders down the phone to the butchers and the fish factors, and occasionally resorted to barefaced threats. If the lambs weren't at the back door within quarter of an hour, then they knew what they could go and do. Even Santos was subdued.

In the hallway the young waiters brought in on emergencies were kitting themselves up. The para familia lunch alone would have to stretch out to feed fifty. I took some of the trays of tapas to the upstairs bar. The front door was wide open. Outside, in the street, the waiters had set up a table on which they placed dishes of chorizo and a large glass drinking vessel full of rosé. The public helped themselves and put in a booking. Two hundred reservations had come in by 11.00 and Duque looked happy. It was a fresh and sunny day, which could only make matters worse for us in the engine room. 'You can cook para familia today, Gisbert. Nothing exotic. To start with, fifty sopa castellana and filete ruso with chips, and a salad. They can have fruit for pudding. You can manage that can't you? Want anything, shout for it. No time for aching today. And when you've finished that you can start singing for your supper, help in any other way you can... salads, soups, other tapas, washing up the pans. Dominga and Rellés will be into it up to their ears. One, two, three, very well fandango. Get down to work... Hey!' Pedro bellowed. 'Big Mouth. What do you think you're doing? Get out of the kitchen, there isn't any space. And you can tell all the waiters now that if they don't form a line they won't get the food.'

This was how I wanted Pedro to treat me, just as one more chef in the overworked kitchen. I grabbed a giant stockpot, put it on the range and filled it full of water with a hose. There was a no point in breaking your back too often trying to lift up a full pot. This was the prelude to the *sopa castellana*. The recipe below is for four. Save this instant soup for a cold winter's day.

2 cups olive oil
12 cloves garlic
1 tbsp salt
1 tbsp cumin
1 heaped tbsp pimentón dulce (sweet paprika)
1½ litres water
4 poached eggs
200 g jamón serrano, chopped into matchsticks
4 slices day-old white farmhouse bread

Fry eight cloves of garlic in the oil until golden brown and discard. Pound up the salt, the remaining four cloves of garlic and cumin in a pestle and mortar, and fry. Add the pimentón, stir for a minute and strain the oil into the water which should be at a rolling boil. Stir. In individual earthenware crocks first place a slice of the bread and on top the poached egg sprinkled with ham. Pour on the stock. Serve.

One of the key factors in this dish, as in most Castilian cooking, is the choice of paprika. There are many different varieties and strengths. In the butchers they often sell them loose and the ultramarinos will always have a good range in tins. The high consumption of paprika is probably the single most important reason, after exercise, why every Castilian peasant doesn't fall down dead with a coronary before the age of forty. The Hungarian Nobel prizewinner, Professor Albert Szent-Gyorgyi, gave overwhelming proof of paprika's extremely high Vitamin A and C content, which can only be helpful to those who survive solely on a pork and bread diet.

Pedro looked pleased with my progress. The fifty crocks were ready and waiting, the salads composed, the chips ready for a final fry and all I had to make now was 150 filetes rusos, uncomplicated, breadcrumbed, flat hamburgers. The only problem was time but Pedro mucked in with me. His agility and familiarity with the process speeded things up.

'Keep good control of the order board and take off the orders from the first sitting before adding the next, otherwise we'll get into all kinds of trouble. And don't sing. SCREAM.'

The chefs' lunch consisted of whatever was closest to hand: a fried egg, a slice of ham on bread, or the leftovers from the staff lunch. Jojo was in a panic. He had to be in two places at once, alongside Clemente roasting lamb and downstairs basting cochinillo. It was the best training possible for the preparation of army food. Mariano was everywhere – peeling vegetables, preparing extra tortillas, helping Pedro carving up T-bones and beef tenderloins. It was the first day that there was no space on the ranges for the open skillets of oil for deep frying and the electric deep-frier was switched on. I think the chefs distrusted this modern intrusion into the kitchen but it would have to be used anyway. Félix had started a small pan fire and with a puff of breath blew it out. The kitchen was filled with acrid smoke and with tears running from our eyes we all choked for a minute or two. The windows were thrown wide open, the extractor fan switched to full and we waited out in the hall. Pedro, Mariano and Clemente worked on regardless.

By three we were up to 400 orders and the first shift had left. I was sent to fetch another carafe of wine for the chefs and stopped to have a look how things were going in the upstairs bar. Duque and Julián were standing in the door noting down table numbers. The queue stretched a hundred yards down calle Réal and ample use was being made of the glass wine carafe. I ran down into the kitchen for more chorizo.

'Lively up there, is it?' questioned Mariano. 'Gisbert, get us all a cup of coffee.' It was too hectic to contemplate being tired. At six in the evening the last couple sat down to start their lunch. They had lapped Segovia's restaurants several times but it was just as bad everywhere else. One thing was for certain, they weren't driving back to Madrid without eating their ration of cochinillo. Compared to the golden piglet, all of Segovia's other historical monuments paled to insignificance. Even the 2,000-year-old aqueduct was nothing when compared to it; it was just a front door to the city.

By eight o'clock we were dead on our feet. The pinches still had the worst task of the day ahead of them, the scrubbing of the ovens. I walked home slowly. Pedro hadn't said so, but I thought I had won my first stripe.

The remaining few days till Easter were quiet in the restaurant. All the activity switched to the church. In every parish the faithful were preparing themselves for the most important day in their calendar, Good Friday.

We had made an arrangement to meet Asún, another doctor who also worked out in the villages. We phoned to confirm. She couldn't meet up that night, she was sorry. Well, what about on Good Friday and we could watch the processions together? Asún was more than disinclined. She was getting out of Segovia. The Easter processions reminded her of everything her generation was trying to forget. The Church and Franco walked hand in hand. It was a morbid spectacle, just like bullfighting. And it reeked of the past. You should see it once, she told us. But once is enough. She was going to take her children down to the beach. With four days off, why stay in Segovia?

Millions of madrileños had reached the same conclusion as Asún. Easter was a holiday. On the news they were warning drivers of the dangers of 'Operation Exit'. It would start on Thursday morning and they would keep a running total on the death toll. By Friday lunchtime there were usually more than fifty dead. Apart from the traffic that poured through Segovia it was relatively quiet out on the street. People were staying indoors. By seven in the evening all that had changed as the city got ready for the Easter procession. In the plaza there was no room to move. So we took up a privileged position on the first-floor balcony at Las Columnas. Pepe (the young chef)'s girlfriend, Marie Cruz, was going to be in the procession. She was the sister of Maribel, the laundry girl at Duque's. For them at least it was a deadly serious occasion. A police car rolled forward slowly through the crowd.

'They're on the way,' shouted Jesús, Pepe's elder brother. We could already hear the hypnotic drumbeat and the wailing lament of the dulzaina. On either side of the street the hooded penitents, all in the same maroon costume, marched slowly forward in time with the drums. Their Ku Klux Klan hoods looked horribly menacing. I could understand Asún's misgivings but it was more frightening than that; its roots went back even earlier than Franco to the powerful religious orders of the Templars, the Order of Malta, and the knights of Calatrava, Talavera and Santiago. It was a scene straight out of the Spanish Inquisition. The first float rolled slowly forward. On top was the lifesize polychrome image of Christ in the Garden.

'Not bad,' commented an elegant elderly lady seated at my side. 'But it's not my favourite. There are others that are far more beautiful. The one from my barrio is probably the best of all.' Behind the image the serious penitents followed. Some went barefoot, others held out their arms in the position of the cross, while many heaved along heavy crucifixes on their shoulders. One of them was made from railway sleepers and the penitent struggled painfully to drag it along, stumbling every few steps.

Patricio, the wild poet of the streets, had tied together two sticks and was walking his own particular road to Calvary.

Earlier on in the day he had addressed an improvised poem to his barrio's image which had reduced many in the multitude to floods of tears. The drum beat continued relentlessly.

'What barrio do you come from?'

'Santa Eulália.'

'Ah! Well, there's a fine image for you. It's in my top three.'

The images came past one by one, describing the Passion as they went. The strangest of all was the Guardia Civil's catafalque. At each corner luminous green flames leapt up high in the air throwing off scented smoke. The Guardia Civil stood guard on either side in their elegant dress uniforms. They marched slowly forward with military precision. I felt divorced from, and at the same time horribly fascinated by, what was passing in front of my eyes. The grief seemed totally authentic. It was as if we were present at the actual Crucifixion, not just watching a cartoon passage through its highlights. The monotonous and relentless drumbeat drowned out any sense of time. Perhaps here was a key to understanding Spain. But it was a riddle without an answer. It was moving, beautiful and vulgar all at once – religion as a form of display. The Church was expressing fully its power and organization; and the idea of a man or woman enjoying an individual relationship with their God was impossible to imagine during this essentially communal experience.

'Here she comes now,' cried Jesús, 'fetch Pepe out of the kitchen to see his sweetheart.'

Marie Cruz was marching with the Gascones. She was one of the three dark beauties, walking like Egyptian mummies, in front of the image. But there was not a hint of vanity in their performance. Marie Cruz never once looked up towards our window. They were there as prime examples of Spanish womanhood, obedient in their mourning. In their outstretched hands they coyly held replicas of the shroud – the veronica. It was a sign language that every Catholic Spaniard would readily understand. During the procession, quirky details brought you back to earth: the drummers that missed a beat, the designer trainers that peeped out from under the capes and the penitents in costume trying to trip each other up.

One of the last images was the most powerful of all, a classic masterpiece of the Spanish school of realist polychrome sculpture: a recumbent Christ by the master, Gregorio Hernández. It was a perfect demonstration of the art of super-realism. The deposition had just passed by. Christ was finally at rest, the blood drained from his body. His sores suppurated. It was morbid and macabre, leaving nothing to the imagination, a final hymn to man's frailty and death.

Our only response was to order our favourite tapas. The images marched on to the beat of the drum.

GATEWAY OF THE CATHEDRAL, SEGOVIA.

5: Easter Sunday

Easter Sunday is the day for an outing, time to celebrate the end of Lent. Around Segovia there are many castle towns: Coca, Turégano, Cuéllar, Pedraza and Sepúlveda. All of them are worth a visit. Like most of the merchant palaces of Segovia, these fortified strongholds were built on the profits from the wool trade. That was back in the early Middle Ages; since then almost all of rural Spain has been in steady decline. But at least two of the towns, Pedraza and Sepúlveda, had managed to reverse their bad fortune by specializing in the roasting of milk-fed lamb. It is the Easter Sunday treat.

The countryside outside Segovia was changing all the time as it slowly recovered from the drought of the previous summer. Livid greens and yellows had finally replaced the burnt ochres and browns of before. The storks on the church towers were becoming more active, repairing their nests and preparing for their young. And along every roadside, the wild flowers had exploded into a feast of bright colour. Acres of poppies and cornflowers stretched out in the distance while overhead the vultures kept guard. They slowly circled around until they saw a dead sheep or dog and then plummeted down to gorge themselves. At times they became so sated they could hardly take off and loped along like clumsy dinosaurs trying to effect an escape. Along the roadside there were kitti-hawks and kites out hunting, waiting for the fieldmice to break across the tarmac. Sometimes, when no village was in sight, the landscape looked like the steppes of Georgia or the prairies of the Mid-West.

We stopped off in Turégano to buy a loaf of bread. The town crier was standing in the square wearing his official peaked cap. He blasted on his horn and shouted out his message:

'Citizens of Turégano. By order 648 of the town-council statutes, the leaking drain in the Plaza de España is to be mended at the council's expense as soon as is physically possible. Further to this, the lightning conductor on the castle, which recently took a direct hit, will, by order 124-5, be mended.'

There was a queue outside the baker's. All the village was waiting patiently to hand over their earthenware dishes of lamb. The baker would roast it for them after his second batch of bread. Each person was given a lottery ticket and a time for collection. By the time I was served the numbers were into treble figures. It was the best way, the villagers said, to cook the lamb.

The baker's recipe for the *cordero asado* is simple, relying on the top quality and freshness of the milk-fed lamb. No herbs are necessary, as the ewes have spent their life feeding off wild thyme, lavender and other fragrant scrubs. The quantities are, as to be expected, enormous. This recipe is for two.

1 shoulder lamb with end ribs
1 leg lamb
Salt
Glass of water

Put in an earthenware dish and roast in a medium oven for two hours. Baste with the juices. Serve. The Segovian style of lamb is so that the meat is tender but almost falls off the bone. It is accompanied by a plain, sharply dressed salad, plenty of bread and a carafe of cool Ribera de Duero rosé.

Back at Duque's it was relatively peaceful. Now was the time, Marisa told me, to prepare her a trifle. The excuses had gone on for long enough. After lunch she would come down into the kitchen and we would get down to it. I had tried to sidestep the subject over the last few weeks but Marisa was persistent. I didn't want to put Pedro's nose out of joint. I was there to learn from him; and apart from that I had never made a trifle. I suspected it might turn into a performance.

Marisa had the whole kitchen on the hop. Sponge cake. 'Pedro, some sponge cake.' Sweet sherry. 'Mariano, run up and get Gisbert some vintage sweet sherry.' It wasn't going down well. 'Rellés, wash out a glass salad bowl for Gisbert's masterpiece.' The landlady's trifle must have been something special. I was generous with everything, but the sherry above all. You could have got drunk on the dish. The time came to put the trifle in the fridge and Marisa retired upstairs. I apologized to Pedro.

'Hombre. It's nothing. Apologise for what? Marisa's got a sweet tooth. She loves any kind of pudding.'

I stood in the washing-up room chatting to Dominga.

'You're coming to the party next week, aren't you? Fernando's leaving us to go into the mili. We're all having dinner out together, a few drinks, and then on to the disco. But you're not allowed to bring your wife. I'm not bringing my husband. It's a staff-only party.' Of course I would, it was bound to be fun.

Santos had hurt his hand lifting a pan and it was bandaged up tightly. Could I, he asked, help him fry some chips? Nothing easier, I'll do it right now. On the range the wide pan of smoking oil was ready for use. I had worked in most of the different stations now and was beginning to feel confident. It wasn't so difficult. I picked up a large handful of chips, drained them between my fingers and walked purposefully over to the stove. There was nothing in the kitchen I couldn't cope with. I swung my arm forward nonchalantly and let the chips fly.

'No, Gisbert! No!' Santos yelled. Everything went into painful slow motion. The chips spun round in the air as they flew straight to their mark. Clemente was bent down under the hot plate basting a lamb. The chips sunk into the oil and as they submerged the boiling oil swelled up slowly like lava, broke through its skin and leapt straight out of the pan. Giant tear drops fell on the hot plate and exploded into flame but others reached further and fell on Clemente's arm. He leapt up and dropped the lamb.

'Hostias. ¡La hostia!' His eyes spat fire. If there was any time suitable for addressing the Host, it was now. Clemente leapt around in severe pain, rubbing his arm. 'What the hell happened there?' Clemente shouted in anger. Normally he was the quietest of men, controlled and composed even when driven to the absolute limit by Santos's incessant stream of jokes. But I had found his weak spot. He didn't like pain.

'Quick, Clemente! Get your arm in cold water,' Pedro urged. The skin on his arm was coming up in angry red bubbles. He couldn't bear to look at me. I apologised to him.

'Clemente, I'm sorry. I'm incredibly sorry. I won't do it again.' You're too right you won't, I could see flashing across his mind. Pedro went over to the first-aid box, and took out some cream and bandage. He was the kitchen's resident doctor. Santos looked at me sternly and started to speak.

'Don't ever do that again. It's madness. I know you haven't worked in a kitchen for long but that was bloody stupid. It isn't just that you burnt Clemente's arm, though that's bad enough.' Clemente looked at me as if to say, it's all right now, you've learnt your lesson. And what's a burnt arm? An occupational hazard. Let's not make a scene out of this. But Santos hadn't finished. 'If a large drop of that oil had gone in Clemente's eye you could have blinded him. And you could have burnt down the restaurant in a gigantic pan fire and us along with it.' Santos tailed off, he knew it had been a moment's aberration. 'Come to think of it' – a smile broke out at the corners of his mouth – 'if you had burnt Clemente's face it could only have been an improvement. Hey, Clemente, look at it this way: Gisbert was trying to do you a favour. You should be grateful.' Clemente didn't look it but the bitter edge had been rubbed off by Santos's humour. I certainly had learnt my lesson. There were some basic rules in the kitchen so simple you hardly needed to think about them; for me, they hadn't yet become second nature.

'Don't worry about it,' Clemente reassured me. 'I'm always burning myself. At home I've got a kiln. I make ceramics, you see. It's my hobby. Painted tiles and vases, and things like that. If you want, you can come over to the village and have a look, any day you want.'

In the evening we met up for drinks with friends at La Concha. This is the hub of Segovian social life; if you wait long enough, almost everyone passes through at one time or another. An Englishman once told me a story about a Spanish friend of his. The Spaniard had come to London for a few days' break but wanted to surprise his friend rather than phone. He went to Piccadilly Circus and waited two days for his friend to pass through, gave up and travelled home back to Spain.

The waiters at La Concha, and Soto at Negresco next door, serve drinks, but also provide a message service. Borrowed car keys and plans for the evening are checked in behind the bar. In the first few months we would make strict plans and arrangements with all our new friends. But after a while it dawned on us that this was redundant, a waste of a call. All one had to do was to stand at La Concha from two to half-past, or from eight in the evening till no later than nine. News on dinners, cinemas, parties, theatre and concert events filter through here and, naturally, the ones who know where everyone is are Jai and Soto. Both may be standing behind the bar serving you but the divide is meaningless; more than anyone else, they have a licence to comment on your actions from the evening before. There are hundreds of cliques, spoilt friendships and sworn enemies in Segovia but for the little time they are in the bar they cohabit in peace. The touchstones are Jai and Javier El Soto.

Jai came past where I was sitting on my own.

'You're like an owl, you know, always watching, always attentive.' If I was the owl, he was the eagle; he could spot an empty glass across the plaza. It was like sitting outside a Paris café watching the world go by. The clothes-conscious Spaniards love their parade and La Concha was a small microcosm of all the latest fashions, a poseurs' paradise. There was Segovia's solitary punk with beer bottle in hand, the Sloane Ranger whose teddy bear wore her Piaget watch, a Cure Head, a Rockabilly, a Glam Queen and many more. There was further entertainment provided by the two middle-aged 'walking women', Guadalupe and her sidekick. They were a Segovian institution and knew the gossip on everyone. Guadalupe strode through the streets shouting out information.

'There he is, the one over there, bald as a coot. He's pretending not to notice. Well, he should keep a better eye on things, like his father, otherwise he'll find himself a cuckold.' Outside La Concha were her richest pickings and those with skeletons in the cupboard were terrified by her tirades. She had nothing on me, so I felt safe. But that evening she had fitted me in and found me a role. 'Look at that one. He's always grinning. It's hardly surprising, though. Look at him' – pointing me out – 'the gynaecologist. He's always trying to put his hand where he shouldn't.' Her silent partner nodded in agreement.

Duque walked passed the kitchen and nodded hello.

'Strange dish, the treeflee (the trifle). We had it for supper last night. It was very tasty but more like a soup than a cake. In England it must be a summer speciality. Like a sweet gazpacho with bread floating in it.'

I went to the fridge and looked inside. They had eaten half of it but what was left was a runny slush of jelly and cream: a complete failure. In my attempt to outdo the Sussex landlady I had forgotten that two schooners of strong sweet sherry counter all the jelly's effects. Later in the morning I went to fetch something out and the level of the trifle soup had gone down. By lunchtime it had vanished.

The temperature was now slowly creeping up to the 70's; one freakishly warm day, it leapt up into the 80's. The diet was changing and I noticed that the demand for stews had fallen off. More fish was being ordered and, in particular, the speciality, *trucha segoviana*, an excellent way of dealing with the mild flavour of farmed trout.

'You've told your wife, I suppose, about Fernando's party. She's letting you go, isn't she?' Dominga asked anxiously

'Yes,' I replied, 'don't worry, Dominga, I'm looking forward to it. I haven't been to a disco in years. I like a dance.'

Everyone in the kitchen was in a high state of excitement. The cycling epic, the Tour of Spain – La Vuelta – had just started and Segovia's favourite son, Pedro Delgado – Perico – was in a good position to win. His photo was everywhere. The previous year he had won the Tour de France and the city had celebrated in style. All the restaurants had set out tables of food under the aqueduct awaiting Perico's arrival by helicopter. But the crowd had lost all its composure as he came into view. Tables were turned over in the rush to get closer to him and the food was plastered onto the cobbles. It had ended in chaos.

Perico had also been at the art-school party during carnival, but disguised as a blackamoor he had escaped the attentions of the crowd. The secret of his success, of course, has a typically Segovian explanation. It's all down to the diet. What else would you expect from someone who was brought up on generous helpings of cochinillo and lentils? A racing cyclist. It was obvious.

His rags-to-riches story is every schoolboy's dream. The adults have their own version of this, the Lottery. Hardly a single day passes without the phrase 'When I win the lottery'. It is a national disease. Everyone buys tickets. The likelihood of a winner saying 'It won't change my life' is a million to one. It is the only reason for playing. A new car, a new house and never having to work again are what fuel the passion for this hobby. Generous gestures towards the family and friends are planned with the financial rigour normally associated with a multinational's five-year plan. Aunts and uncles will be cared for, father will get his Mercedes, younger brother the bicycle of his dreams and mother her kitchen refitted.

The chefs in the kitchen bought their tickets, from the one-armed ticket salesman, almost every day. If they won, you could bet your bottom dollar it would be the last time they stepped through Duque's door. They might even buy a restaurant of their own. It made sound business sense. Segovia is the city in Spain with most bars per head of population – one for every eighty inhabitants. No one here had ever lost a penny serving up food, they averred. But it was blatantly untrue. The bar opposite our house had just folded the week before. It was the military changing room where the conscripts came to slip into casual clothes before a night on the town. They were about the only clients and one drink at the beginning and end of the night came nowhere near to paying the overheads.

Duque called me on the intercom. There were two friends upstairs waiting for me in the bar. Mon and Rafael, an inseparable pair of painters, had come to check me out. I had told them the week before that I worked in Duque's and they didn't believe a word of it. The moment they saw me they broke into hysterical laughter.

'I shit in the sea. It's true.' Tears were rolling down their cheeks. 'It's too much. Just too much.'

From down in the kitchen the war cry went up.

'He's escaped. He's escaped.' Who? 'Perico, of course, he's left them for dead.' We were proud to be Segovians.

I walked home to the flat. Up the stairwell I could smell all sorts of delicious aromas. The front door of each of the flats had an elegant circular brass grille set into it, an early nineteenth-century form of ventilation. And on the way up to the second floor I could work out what our neighbours were having for their lunch: chicken with garlic, grilled fish, or pungent, saffron-flavoured paella. Downstairs the husbands were all sitting in the bar enjoying their pre-lunch wine with a snack.

Boni and Sagrario had been working hard on my wife's culinary education and they still couldn't believe that she didn't do all the cooking. All the specialist shops had been pointed out to her because naturally it had to be her who did all the food shopping as well. We bumped into them at the Thursday market. I was carefully going over the lettuce. That one's got a good heart, I said, I'll have that. Boni picked it up and inspected it sceptically. What does he know?

'Is that the one you want, Alejandra?' asked Sagrario. She wasn't about to let me browbeat my wife into making a reckless impulse purchase. Boni peeled back the mottled outside leaves and pinched at the pale green heart, 'You certainly know how to shop, Gisbert.' But I could see that she put it down to chance.

All kinds of new things had come into the market. One of the most exciting were the baskets full of *cardillos* – golden thistle stalks – that looked like a small frisée salad. Swiss chard was also prominent and there were plastic bags of small green peppers, *pimientos de Padrón*. Be careful with those, Sagrario warned, some of them are very, very hot. There was no way of telling, although Pedro claimed you could do it by smell. I couldn't and the chefs had had a funny half hour watching me dousing the fire with litres of wine. I had prepared the cardillos for the first time in the way you'd expect, with a vinaigrette. But they were too tough to eat. In Castile, they are cooked as a vegetable and make for a good hearty first course.

1 kilo cardillo
1 thick slice jamón serrano
1 small chorizo
2 tbsp olive oil
Salt
Cup of water
1 tbsp chopped parsley
4 cloves garlic

Boil the cardillo in a pan of salted water until tender. Drain. Cut the jamón serrano into tiny blocks and the chorizo into thin slices. Fry in the olive oil along with the sliced cloves of garlic for a few minutes. Turn up the heat to full. Throw in the cardillos and the glass of water. Stir. Season. Sprinkle with the parsley and serve. The acelgas – Swiss chard – can be treated in the same way but I often employ a non-Castilian trick of enlivening the dish with the juice of half a lemon.

Fernando's last day, before doing his stretch in the army, had come. He hardly needed to work and by the end of lunch it would have been dangerous to let him anywhere near a knife. Santos and the waiters had spiked his glass with anything that might go unnoticed in red wine. Everyone in the kitchen was happy, except Fernando, who was on the brink of leaving Segovia for the first time in his life. He had really come to think of the Duque staff as his extended family, and for the first few days at least, he would be lost without us.

I had often seen him walking the streets at night with Jojo and Pototo, and now the trio of pinches was going to be split up.

'You'll never come back and work in Duque's,' said Jojo.

'You might meet a nice Arab girl, marry, have a family and settle down.' Santos chipped in.

'Don't smoke too many herbal cigarettes, Fernando. The wacky backy stunts your growth.'

Mariano had prepared us all breaded veal cutlets. Fernando was given a special treat, a prime fillet steak. 'Tonight you and Pedro are going to be de Rodriguez,' Rellés told me – a Spanish saying for a family man out on his own. And Dominga and Rellés had planned to spend the afternoon at the hairdresser's. It was going to be a big night.

In the afternoon break we attempted an English class but our minds were on other things. Fernando was sent home early. For the first time in two years he was excused from the torture of scrubbing the stoves. He needed his siesta.

At eight o'clock we all met in Duque's downstairs bar and trudged down the hill to the bars in the barrio Carmen. A giant glass porrón of beer was ordered for all of us. It is a difficult ritual. The fine dribble of beer comes out of the spout and arcs like a fountain through the air. It's regarded as bad form to put your mouth round the spout. It's hard, and for a beginner impossible, not to end up soaking your shirt. That's half the fun. The real aficionados hold the porrón at arm's length and project the first gush straight into their open mouth. The flow is kept going and the arm extended further and further away. You have to try and swallow with your mouth wide open. I made a fool of myself a couple of times but gradually mastered the art.

'Another porrón!' Santos shouted. 'Next size up!' Dominga and Rellés giggled in the corner. The porrón was heavy and held six pints. 'Now I'll show how you really do it,' Santos boasted. 'I learnt it in the army, Fernando. It's a useful trick.'

We all moved back and gave Santos room. He picked up the porrón and hoisted it into the air. The first jet of beer hit the tip of his tongue. Not a drop was spilt. Jojo and Pototo started to clap. Santos smiled and leant back further. The stream of beer looked like a rainbow. He teased the liquid over his teeth, onto his tongue and swallowed deeply. Concentrating hard, he lifted the porrón even higher and the fine fountain moved onto his top lip. He slowly worked up along the side of a nostril and on to the bridge of his nose – and still the beer trickled down into his mouth. Moving up his nose he crossed between his eyebrows and onto his forehead.

Not a single drop was spilt. We broke into rapturous applause.

'And now, Gisbert, it's your turn.'

'You've got to be joking!' But he wasn't. Santos had downed almost a litre of beer. I wasn't going to be a killjoy, so I launched the porrón up in the air. There was no way my hand was steady enough to follow the long and winding road up my nose. So I took a short cut from my open mouth straight up to my forehead, via my eyes. As a sensation it wasn't unpleasant. It was a warm night outside. But very little of the beer got into my mouth. Most of it went running down under my collar and over my tie. To judge by the applause it was deemed a total success but for the rest of the night I was horribly sticky.

As a party piece it was often practised at bullfights by the serious fans in *tendido* 7. They would pour their wine from the leather pig bladders and offer it round. Drunkeness, however, was not the final aim – unlike the English, Santos said, whom he had seen on the south coast. What's wrong with them? All the time I had been at Duque's I dreaded this subject coming up. But summer was only two months away and I sensed it as a brooding presence, something that one day would have to be explained away. Along with appalling English food, it is one of the stock clichés for the Spanish. I couldn't talk from experience but it was at moments like this, and whenever England played Spain at football, that I pleaded diplomatic immunity and sheltered behind my Dutch nationality.

'They aren't any better,' Santos riposted, 'they're all thugs too. But they're better at football. Just look what a disaster El Tel made of Barcelona. Thank God for Cruyff. Mind you, it's not easy working with Catalans. They've got their hand in your purse before you can even turn round.'

'You couldn't, it's true, imagine a night like this in Catalonia. It would be too complicated. They would have their pocket calculators out, trying to work out how much Santos had to pay for that last pull on the porrón.'

'Here in Castile we're more generous. We're born, we die, we're all human and worthy of respect. In the end we're all the same.' What about Perico's performance today (we were safer back on Segovian soil)? 'The man's a genius! He opened his shoulders, showed them his face, displayed his balls and stuck it up their arse.'

Our next staging post before the disco was Segovia's only Italian restaurant. For a party it served its purpose but its fare looked suspiciously like Castilian food. The disco was fun and as we were pretty well the only clients we did our best to send Fernando off to the army with memories to sustain him through the dog days in the desert.

The following morning we all met up again at work. It wasn't the same, was it, without Fernando? Life was like that in the kitchen. The staff was always changing.

'Today, Gisbert, you're changing job. We're sending you over to the Floresta palace with Mariano. There's a big wedding on.'

The Floresta palace is Duque's banqueting hall used for receptions, fashion shows, council meetings and weddings. May, in Segovia, is the favourite month for couples to tie the knot, La Floresta the most stylish venue. It is a restored fifteenth-century aristocrat's home that was finally abandoned during the Civil War. Duque spent years restoring it and then passed it over to Marisa. It was her baby, and over the last few weeks we had seen her less and less as the season was picking up.

The true Segovian wedding is a practical, democratic affair, contradicting everything that had been pinpointed as the Segovian character only the evening before. When Segovians get married they become honorary Catalans for the day. A month before the wedding, invitations are sent out; firm replies are appreciated. The wedding takes place in the bride's barrio, or village, and then everyone transports himself to La Floresta. Few presents are given because at the end of the meal everyone goes Dutch and pays their corner. If the bill comes to 3,000 a head then it's normal to round it up to 5,000, or 10,000 if feeling generous. The extra money pays for the honeymoon and the furnishing of the first house. If the couple can't afford a flat and are going to stay on living with the in-laws, then the money is banked in the *caja* until there's enough to put down a deposit. It's a sensible way of organising things and when I told Mariano that the bride's father usually paid for everything in England, he looked horrified. It compounded his suspicions that Northern Europe was a society of millionaires. The Segovian system means that even the poorest couple, as long as they are blessed with loyal friends, are sent off in style.

The wedding menu is almost always the same: a plate of meats to start off with; an intermediate course of asparagus with mayonnaise, or giant tiger prawns; and then the pièce de résistance – a perfect cochinillo, served up with full pomp and circumstance, and carved with a plate.

'You know why Pedro sent you to work over here today,' said Mariano. No. I hadn't seen the Floresta palace before and because it was a quiet day at Duque's, I imagined Pedro was broadening my horizons. 'Today, you're going to put on the toque and dedicate the pig to the newlyweds,' – so, my coming-of-age in the kitchens of Castile. It made me nervous. Weddings are special events, and it seemed a bit unfair to use today's bride and groom as guinea pigs. It was an occasion of important Segovian rituals and I might spoil it for them. Mariano could sense my worries. 'It won't be difficult, Gisbert. I'll be standing next to you, in case anything should happen. We'll have a practice run just before.'

There were going to be more than 400 guests at the reception and we worked to a ratio of one cochinillo for every group of six. We had some serious roasting to do. Compared to Duque's, the kitchens in La Floresta were like walking into a space station. It was spacious and airy; the abundance of white tiles and stainless steel lent it a certain surgical air. It was a good place to work, Mariano told me, but it didn't have the romance of working straight onto the wood-burning stoves. Here everything was run on electricity and gas, was efficient, but something was lost in the process. Mariano didn't mind. He preferred working at La Floresta. You were left more on your own. Of course, it wasn't as creative as working with Pedro, because the wedding menu was strictly limited, but you still had to ensure that eighty suckling pigs reached perfection at exactly the same time, and that wasn't easy. Mariano showed me into the roasting chamber. The oven was enormous, the latest line in commercial bakery equipment brought in from Germany. It was already coming up to the right temperature and Mariano told me to have a look inside. He leant against a large wheel, the size of a yachtsman's helm, and pulled it down with effort. A deep grinding noise started up. The whole stone bed of the oven moved slowly round. That was the major advantage of this modern device and it made the roasting just that little bit easier. Preparing eighty cochinillos was like shuffling a pack of cards and picking out the ace. With the old-style oven down in Duque's basement, you used long baker's paddles to lift the pigs out. If it was the one furthest away you wanted to turn, or baste, then every other one in its way would have to come out first. Everything took twice as long.

There were two and a half hours left before the meal was to be served, so we began the roasting. Jojo and Félix were laying out the meats, and

Mariano and I started to think of alternatives for the few vegetarians – as well as for the philistines who had phoned up and asked for something else ('anything but yet another piglet'). They were probably worried about their cholesterol levels and high blood pressure, I suggested.

'No,' said Mariano. 'It's just the fashion to complain. It looks more important if you have something the next person doesn't. I can't see the point of a set menu if half of the guests want something else. It's only twenty, but it's enough.'

We settled on the old favourite of *salmón a la plancha* as a standby; and instead of the cured meats we would prepare a vegetable terrine, and everyone would be happy. Down behind the kitchens was a large discothèque and bar the guests could use if they were in the mood for dancing. At five in the afternoon? Just you wait till you see them, warned Mariano. It's amazing what they get up to. At one wedding last year they had a big formal lunch and didn't stop dancing until four in the morning.

The guests arrived on time. We were now awaiting the bride and groom, who would be cheered victoriously up to the top table. It was an occasion for putting on best dresses and reviving old suits. The bride and groom's parents were already sitting down. The grandparents looked as if they had never been to a restaurant before and two of the old men stubbornly kept their berets on. The couple made their entrance and the party began. Mariano and I went down to the kitchen and juggled the cochinillos around in the oven, basting and turning them over, and pricking others with a sharp trident to let the fat run.

I sneaked up the stairs and peeped through the door. The noise was deafening.

'Kiss the bride! Kiss the bride!' they chanted. The bridegroom performed his duty and bread rolls flew in the air. On the table nearest to me a young woman stood up and screamed out '*¡Maricón!*' – slang for homosexual – and pelted a man at the other end of a table with a slice of chorizo. Her parents looked on admiring her spirit. Mariano was behind me and laughed like a drain.

'Let's get the display ready,' he choked. We dressed up the trestle with rosemary and thyme, and in the bottom laid loaves of stale bread. 'It's just a precaution, Gisbert, in case you overdo the trick with the plate and smash the earthenware dish. Come on, let's have a practice.' Mariano picked up a plate and pushed it in my hand. Sharp, powerful blows were needed. Mariano held his hand out like a boxing trainer and told me to strike. 'Remember. Two down the spine and four blows across. Make a meal of it, really camp it up. Then pass the plate on to the bride. When they've cut the meat, she smashes the plate down on the floor. It's simple.' Where did the smashed plate tradition come from?

I asked Mariano. Was it medieval? It was as ancient as the day that one of Cándido's washer-uppers had left a plate greasy. It slipped out of the master's hand and there it was a tradition invented.

It was time. The dulzaina player and drummer led us into the hall. Four hundred faces stared at Mariano and me – a Laurel and Hardy act, with piglets – as we marched down the aisle. Mariano spoke up as I held the plate high in the air with grave authority.

'In the style of Henry IV of Castile...' – and I bludgeoned the beast. 'Three cheers.'

I carried it off well enough and now the wedding reached its gastronomic climax. The arrival of the cochinillos revived the guests' spirits. For the first time the large banqueting ball went quiet as everyone put their heads down and started troughing. For the first few mouthfuls knives and forks were used to tease the flesh from the bone, and to split the delicate crackling into bite-size pieces, but they didn't last long before being abandoned in favour of more active handiwork. Wine bottles emptied and more was called for. The train of waiters was kept on the hop as seconds and thirds were offered up to those who still had room.

When appetites had been finally satisfied the banging on the tables started, accompanied by the clinking sound of cutlery on glass, and the lusty shouts for the bride and groom to kiss once again.

'*¡Beso! ¡Beso! ¡Beso! ¡Beso!*'

The dulzaina and drum joined in again to herald the entrance of the wedding cake. Out came the boxes of cigars and sweets. The bridesmaids and ushers stalked the tables collecting offerings of money in exchange for tiny fragments of the bride's petticoat and the groom's tie that they had hacked off with scissors in the toilets minutes before.

Coffee and brandies were served, and those who still had not had enough started to slip off down the stairs to the discothèque bar where the more serious *cubatas* – long mixers of gin and tonic, and rum and coke – began to be consumed.

Mariano and I retired to the kitchen. Our day was finished. The pinches, waiters and washing-up girls could do all the clearing up.

6: End of the rains

At long last the rains came to an end. On the odd morning there was still a strong white carpet of frost but by eleven after a few hours of sunshine, even that had disappeared. Everyone in the kitchen seemed in a better mood

'It's been a long winter, Gisbert. Far too long. Duque will be happy this morning, you watch. As soon as it warms up a bit all of Madrid will be up here. A nice drive out to La Granja, a walk round the gardens, and then a stroll up the hill from the aqueduct and into Duque's. The foreign coach tours start coming in now as well. Look what I've got for Duque's breakfast this morning.' Pedro signalled to me to follow him to the cold room.

On any normal weekday morning Dionisio Duque would be in by ten. He would stick his head round the kitchen door, say his good mornings and go up into the restaurant for his breakfast over the morning post. Normally Pedro, and it would be only Pedro, would prepare him scrambled egg on toast. An apple blended with yoghurt was another firm favourite. Or if Duque came in slightly later he might decide to have a grilled fillet steak.

Pedro pulled back the handle on the cold room and we walked in. It was the first day that it really felt significantly colder than the outside air. Leaning over to a shelf, Pedro pulled off a small aluminium tapas tray.

'That's what Duque's having for breakfast today,' and he pressed his forefinger and thumb together, brought them up to his lips and exclaimed, '¡Riquísimo!'

I looked into the tray and saw two lambs' heads cleaved in half, just slightly larger than a clenched fist. If Duque was starting the day like this, then God only knew what Pedro had up his sleeve for the boss's lunch.

Back in the kitchen Pedro glanced over to make sure the tapas preparations were on schedule and then focussed on the delicacies in hand.

'A sprinkle of salt, a squeeze of lemon and then a good, fast roast in the oven. We don't want to drown the natural flavour. Oye, Pototo,' barked Pedro in that nasal voice that carried up two floors, remembering something else. 'Why are the dustbins still out by the back door?' Pototo's voice came up from the bar below mumbling something about the saints. Pedro looked at me in disbelief. 'Would you believe it! It's the rubbish collectors' saint's day.'

It sounded quite mad to me. But every type of trade has its patron saint. The chefs' saint's day was only two months away, but that was more of a busman's holiday. All Segovia's chefs get up on the back of open lorries and drive round Segovia serving out food.

I looked at the calendar over Pedro's shoulder and sure enough every single day of the year had a saint. Some were just local, like Segovia's Fuencisla; others were of interest to the trades, like San Antón, the patron saint of butchers; and others of course were national events, like Saragossa's Virgin of the Pillar. Tomorrow's was San Antonio of Padua – an international star – held in particular esteem in Zammaramala, which celebrates the day as a village fiesta.

'It's worth going to see,' said Pedro.

From around the side of the church my attention was drawn by the sound of laughter and excited screams. It was quarter-past six and the bells to signal the start of the service had already rung twice. The view from Zammaramala across the yellowing wheat fields to the Alcázar was stunning in the evening light. Thousands of poppies and cornflowers in the corn suggested that insecticides were not yet in common use.

I put my head round the giant oak doors and peered into the church. Three young children ran out past me straight into the sunny plaza: a ten-year-old boy in a floor-length white cassock, another in a miniature admiral's uniform and a young girl dressed up in a miniature version of a wedding dress. They giggled wickedly when they saw me and tiptoed back into the gloomy interior, then ran out again screaming.

Inside the church the adults seemed oblivious to all the noise. The sound of my footsteps on the flagstones was muffled by a carpet of freshly cut lavender bushes. At the front of the church the priest was busy preparing for the service. Some of the women had already dipped their heads in prayer but most were rapt in animated conversation. It was a high old fiesta atmosphere; the clothes were beautiful and the smell of the lavender was heavenly.

Behind the last pew a large group of children had formed themselves into a circle. One would break from the rest of them move into the middle and then they would all jump back screaming. Four or five times they repeated the game until seeing me they stopped. Their parents ignored them completely. I moved closer and looked in over their heads. Two large sacks lay tied at their feet. Suddenly, the boy in the cassock took a step forward and gave the red netting bag a sharp kick. The package squealed, rolled over clumsily, struggled to stand up, fell over, and squealed loudly again as it stumbled in fits and starts across the floor. The circle opened up as the children nearest the bag ran away. A small boy next to me, unable to contain himself, ran up and down on the spot screaming through his hands.

'Watch out, José! Be careful! Last year's one escaped.'

The fluorescent strip lights went on around the church, the priest tested out the microphone, a man walked down the central aisle towards me, grabbed the tied ends of the two bags and dragged them behind a thick velvet curtain into the annex. Mass began. The maître d' at Duque's, Antonio, was also there. I asked him in a reverent whisper what was going to happen later. He spoke back without lowering his voice:

'San Antonio de Padua.' He pointed to an empty niche, 'Normally he's in there. But now he's up there on the altar, and then later we'll take him for a walk round the village. The Mayor's looking after him today. He's in good hands.'

At the front of the church the small polychrome image of San Antonio de Padua stood on a raised platform with four long handles sticking out from the corners. Around his neck he wore a garland of rosquillas – large hardcrusted doughnuts covered in sticky white icing – on a string. He was placed under a bower of fresh fruits and twisted greenery, set off by the further addition of boiled sweets, miniature bottles of Whisky DYC and Spanish brandies, and a few miniature Nestlé chocolate bars. He had the appearance of a reluctant initiate at a bacchanal.

During the early part of the service the men came in and out of the church as they wished. I joined them under the portico outside. On the far side of the square the small village bar was doing good business. Every so often a head would appear round the door and disappear as quickly. Under the portico the men were catching up on the latest news of their relations who had driven from Madrid and Valladolid for the day. Cigars were lit, arms crossed in anticipation and then the bells in the tower started to ring out their monotonous peal.

The giant doors at the west end of the aisle opened wide and the congregation spilt out into the sunlight. A saxophonist, a drummer and an accordionist struck up a traditional Castilian *jota* – the famous dance of northern Spain – as the priest strode out holding on high a pennant with the image of San Antonio. The saint himself tottered forward slowly above the heads of the crowd. Supported on the shoulders of devotees he crept along, laden down with his kilos of fruit. A pair of old men who had been standing at my side took out the blue bundles from under their arms and unwrapped long rockets. Holding them carefully between finger and thumb they lit the torch paper on their cigars and released them to explode noisily high above the tower. Just a few yards out of the church the procession halted as the weight of San Antonio was passed onto the shoulders of four new parishioners.

Leaving the square the first of the small children, the toddlers and babies, were lifted up for a ride with San Antonio, and allowed to tear off whatever sweet they could reach. Some lapped up all the attention and a chance to gorge themselves, but others found the sea of faces, the music and the few seconds out of their parents' arms too much, and burst miserably into tears. Slowly the triumphal arch over San Antonio's head began to resemble an undressed Christmas tree. At the furthest point out of the village the procession stopped, and everyone looked across the valley to Segovia and admired the view. The weather was perfect. The peaks of the Guadarrama still had a good covering of snow in the deepest of the ravines. Pedro was right, it was worth coming up here to see this – and it was good to be out of the steamy heat of the kitchen.

The procession started up again and joined the main road back into the village. Now it was the adults' turn to steal the show. Two rows of dancers stepped in line in front of the band and facing each other they sidestepped up the road mirroring their partners' tricky steps. San Antonio looked on with his frozen smile. All the way back to the church the spinning crocodile of women kept up their energetic dance. Outside the front door the procession rested for the last time. The Mayor stepped forward:

'Devotees of San Antonio, both women and men, devotees! For the honour of carrying the blessed San Antonio of Padua across the threshold who will give me a price for the handle at the front on the right? 5,000. I have been offered 5,000, up now to 6,000, seven, eight, I am now offered 10,000...' The price closed at 15,000 pesetas. The successful bidder slipped under the long handle and settled the weight in the hollow of her shoulder. Two more corners were sold off quickly, the front left and the back right – another 15,000 each. The final corner, the last chance to make a good impression on the village and the priest, sustained a longer battle. The Mayor coaxed up the price. 'I don't need to point out, loyal devotees of San Antonio, that this trestle has only four corners. Come on, we've reached 22,000. Twenty-two? OK, twenty-two it is.'

First in was San Antonio, followed by the villagers, who filled up all the pews. In the side aisles those who couldn't sit stood ready for what I imagined to be a thanksgiving service, or a moment of prayer. All the men were in the church, but some with cigarettes in their mouths hovered on the threshold, neither in nor out. The bar was empty. The priest walked up to the microphone at the altar and called for quiet. The Mayor took to the stage:

'Devotees of San Antonio of Padua. May we begin?' The village went silent. From a side chapel the Mayor's assistant came across and placed two crystal-clear bottles upon the altar table. They glistened transparently in the light. The priest moved behind the altar as if ready to consecrate the wine and the Host. He nodded to the Mayor his approval. 'Devotees, let's start with a bang. Who is going to give me 4,000 for these two fine bottles of *chinchón*? [Chinchón is a clear, anise-based spirit made in the town of that name south of Madrid.] Best quality. Two-litre bottles of good, dry chinchón. Let's have an offer at 4,000... good. Five... six... seven... do I hear eight?' He paused to heighten the tension and, like any seasoned county auctioneer, followed on: 'I'm giving you once at eight. For the second time at eight. For the last time, I am offered eight for two fine bottles of the very best chinchón. Sold at 8,000.'

The assistant in charge of the lots came out of the chapel and sweeping the church with his eyes picked out the buyer and noted down the name in his makeshift ledger. Jokes were shouted across the aisles on the lines of 'A bottle for you and one for the wife'; the congregation was clearly having fun. Two more bottles were put down next to the cross on the embroidered linen altar-cloth.

'Devotees. Closer to home now. For two bottles of Whisky DYC, what am I offered?' After that, 'Two bottles of a Rioja 1981 – a good harvest. A great vintage. A collector's item.'

He didn't miss a trick. He was ready to advertise the virtues of all the available lots. It moved up to 9,000 and there the bidding faltered. The auctioneer nodded to the underbidder, held up the bottles with a gesture of hopeless resignation and waited. He offered 10,000 pesetas – a hefty price for a pair of bottles you could buy in the shop for 2,000. Crossing the all-important psychological barrier of 10,000 the audience went hush. A large man standing beside me, one of the relations from Madrid, shouted up to the front: 'I'll have them for eleven.' And eleven it was.

The Mayor moved on through the lots, measuring his time, and patiently collected the promises for money on the way to the final special lots. He had already successfully sold seven bottles of assorted spirits, a number of bottles of wine, a five-litre can of stuffed olives and a night out for two, including dinner, at the village restaurant. A factory-made box of biscuits took time to sell, but the crowd was getting more excited by the minute. Pointing to San Antonio he auctioned off one of the chains of homemade rosquillas that hung round his neck. For that he got 7,000 and the next one 6,000. Slowly San Antonio was being undressed in front of his devotees ready to move back to his apse for the coming year, where he would readopt his more sober aspect. Suddenly the excitement increased and all the Mayor's pleadings for silence were completely ignored. The priest moved gravely forwards to the microphone to calm his flock:

'Devotees, please. Please, we must have quiet.'

The children giggled hopelessly as they watched a new-born spring lamb, with a bright blue bow tied round its neck, brought forward for auction. It went for 15,000 and its partner for a couple more.

'Just three more lots to go.' A beautifully hand-wrapped box of rosquillas was placed on the altar. Irregular and delicately painted, they put the competition to shame. I wanted to taste them but when the bidding rose above my ceiling price I had to let them go. Perfect *casera* – 'homemade,' a neighbour told me – from one of the meseta villages close to here. Tomorrow afternoon, when I finished at Duque's, I promised myself I'd come back and find where they were made. Sold for a good price, they were passed over quickly for the moment all the children had been impatiently awaiting.

From round the back one of the assistants dragged out the red netting bag which still let out the occasional grunt, even after all its earlier escape attempts. The string was loosened and out popped the head of a handsome suckling pig. Nothing could have pleased the children more. The piglet looked startled in its noisy surroundings but the adults were already well on the way to beating last year's high price and setting a new auction record.

It was now warm enough to leave the windows wide open at night. It made life easier. The neighbours had got together and decided that life in Segovia was getting too dangerous, so they had a lock fitted to the entrance hall – but forgot we needed bells. If friends came round to visit us at night they couldn't get in. With the windows open, even on the second floor, it felt like living in the street. They just shouted up.

The wind had changed direction and Sahara currents were bringing over clouds of orange dust. Summer, they told me in Bar Prisco, was just a week away. (We were well into one of those roundabout conversations I was getting used to.) One of the regulars would say summer was ten days away, the other a month and the pessimist that he had known it snow in June. By the time I left, the general consensus was for a week; it was obvious that the subject was good for another half hour's heated debate.

The day had been long and tiring. The temperature in the kitchen was stifling. I had drunk far too much of the lemonade and red wine mixture. In the heat you needed to quench your thirst and replace your body fluids every ten minutes. There was something rather absurd about firing up two large wood-burning ovens when the outside temperature was in the 80's. It also made the ovens more difficult to light. For the first twenty minutes, smoke filled the kitchen and finally we had to resort to Clemente's secret weapon, his electric fan. Half an hour later the air was clear but we were up in the 90's. Mariano said it was good training for his mountaineering. The rate at which the ovens were sucking out the oxygen, he reckoned, was the equivalent to a few weeks' altitude training. The hot weather had brought out the customers in droves. I went home and slept deeply.

I was sure I was having a nightmare, one of those that catches you in half-sleep and doesn't want to go away. I had bells ringing in my ears – not deep, resonant church bells but of a higher pitch, and not just two or three but hundreds. They disappeared slowly into the distance and left behind only the occasional echo. I looked up at the alarm clock. It was five in the morning. I dozed off. And back came the bells, carried gently on the warm breeze – first of all dim and distant, and then gradually closer until under the window, down in the street, I could hear hundreds of them again. The dull noise bounced off the walls and rose up to the glass balcony. They sounded like sheep bells.

I got up, rushed out onto the balcony and there they were – a whole flock of sheep coming up from the direction of the aqueduct, going the wrong way up a one-way street. Pushing and bumping into each other, they squeezed their way round the parked cars. A few goats jumped up on the wall of the artillery academy and started stripping away the ivy. The shepherd shouted at his dogs, which moved in fast, weaving through the maze of sheep's legs, and started nipping at the goats' ankles. The sheep had all been recently shorn, clipped back uniformly to resemble some widely ribbed corduroy. On their backs they all carried the identical marking, an ochre circle crossed with a horseshoe. The shepherd marched towards me. His face was a deep, leathery brown, weathered by months on the open meseta. Over his shoulder he carried a folded cream and brown check blanket, and in his hand a long stick. Alongside him shambled five or six other dogs, none of which were from a recognizable breed: half mastiff-half collie, half retriever-half terrier, half Scottie-half Alsatian; it was only to be guessed at. I looked the other way at the sheep that had run on ahead. A lorry was waiting down in the plaza Muerte y Vida to get past and they had surrounded it, grinding it to a standstill. It was one of the early fish trucks that had driven through the night down from Vigo, on the north-west coast in Galicia. He waited patiently until all the sheep had passed and then drove up past the flat belching exhaust fumes in his wake. I went back to bed and again fifteen minutes later the bells came back. Another flock was driven past. This continued with short intervals until eight in the morning. It was hopeless trying to sleep, so I went down to the bar round the corner for hot chocolate and some freshly fried churros. The street was covered in droppings. Literally thousands of sheep and goats had passed by over the last two hours. Why and where to?

I had to wait till Bar Prisco opened to ask Tomás, the owner, my best source for local gossip, folklore and customs, what was going on.

'What was all the commotion this morning?'

'Sheep,' replied the man leaning heavily on the bar.

'What were they doing?'

'Walking.'

Segovians can sometimes be very literal. A friend who fancied his Spanish was sent off one morning to the baker for our morning bread. There was a choice of five or six different types. Choosing the most exotic he asked the baker, 'So what do you call this kind of bread?' A pregnant silence followed. 'Bread,' the baker replied. First names are also a good indicator of this tendency. A very common name in Segovia for the first son is 'First', with the second son named accordingly 'Second'. I know of one very fat man whose name is Mr. Fat; I've seen it on his official identity card. He must have grown into his name.

I wasn't giving in so easily.

'Where are they going?'

'To the train station.'

'They're going to be slaughtered in Madrid then?'

'No, no, no. They're transhumant. Haven't you ever heard the wonderful Castilian song...?' He cleared his throat:

'*Ya se van los pastores...*

The shepherds are going away
to Extremadura.
The sierra is now left
sad and deserted.

The shepherds are going away
off towards the sheepfold.
The sierra is now left
sad and silent.

For the next few days there'll be sheep coming up here every morning. It's a *cañada*, is *Muerte y Vida*, the sheep have right of way. Don't you remember on the news a couple of weeks ago seeing all the pigs on the M30 motorway? Well, that's a cañada too. It was the farmers protesting against the EEC.'

I went to Antonio Ruiz, the local town historian and authority on these matters, who explained everything.

The wool trade is what made Segovia. Every palace, church or monument that dates from after the twelfth century was the product of this trade. The granite and sandstone walls were built on wool. Without sheep, the Golden Age would probably not have happened. To the Castilian economy it was worth more than all the gold from Peru. So quite naturally the trade became highly organized and the different grazing lands fell under the same control. As early as 1273 Alfonso the Wise of Castile tried to rationalize the trade. The sheep trails – the cañadas, and their offshoots, the *veredas* and *cordeles* – were strictly mapped out and became the rightful grazing land for the shepherds in transit. Last June, another friend later explained, the stationmaster at Segovia had spent all his free time tending and preparing a beautiful little garden on the station forecourt. With the first flock of sheep the garden vanished; the sheep had eaten the lot. He was furious but there was nothing he could do. It was a cañada, after all.

In the last few decades, it has changed a lot. The shepherds used to walk the whole way to Extremadura, a round trip of close on 1,000 miles, but now they go by train. Segovia, however, is still ideally situated for the shearing which happens at roughly mid-journey in late spring.

The twenty-third of June is the night of San Juan, one of the biggest days in the shepherd's calendar, Miguel Angel, a carpenter and amateur anthropologist, told me. While the rest of Segovia celebrates the first day of the longest fiesta of the year, eight days and nights of dancing, the shepherd is busy separating the lambs from their mothers in order to strengthen them.

'If you're interested in good food you ought to go out to the sierra, find a shepherd and persuade him to make you *caldereta* (a spicy lamb stew). I know of one in Navafría, Leandro Martín, who is famous throughout the province.

I took Miguel Angel's advice and went off up into the foothills searching for the shepherds. If you keep your eyes and ears open, it isn't long before the shepherd and his flock are located by the telltale signs of the dust cloud, the sound of the muted brass bells, or by the lazy flight of circling vultures.

I had a memorable conversation with one of the shepherds I met. He stood behind a tree with his mule, which was loaded with presents for his family, woollen blankets, waterproofs, a pig's bladder full of wine and the *caldera* (cauldron), patched and burnt black with use. For the past month, like his father, and his father before him, he had covered an average of fifteen and a half miles a day, a total of almost 500 miles. It is a strange experience talking to people so dislocated from what we know as the modern world, and here they seemed thick on the ground. At one point in the conversation he became animated:

'Where are you from?'

'London. London, in England.'

He shook his hand, in disbelief and horror at gigantic distances he couldn't comprehend.

'Ah, yes. I have a brother who went to live a long way away, close to London, I think.'

'Oh, where does he live?'

'Buenos Aires.'

He sat down, opened his bag and offered to share his lunch. With his clasp knife he started to cut up a length of dried chorizo, sweating mousetrap cheese and bread the consistency of concrete. No caldereta. Leandro would be the safest bet.

Leandro said he would do his best to prepare a decent caldereta. So a few days later we went up the mountain to a deserted village where there was enough shade at midday to stop the meal and its preparation becoming a torture. In summer when shepherds meet up they make a party of it and cook caldereta in the shade of a tree. In winter they huddle around the open fire of a *refugio* – a small stone hut built in the mountains, a safe haven in case of the frequent blizzards – to eat their warming and tasty stew. It really is the kind of dish to put the heat back into your bones. For eight years Leandro lived in a refugio, hidden away in the pine forests alongside a trout stream, until his children were old enough to go to school.

Caldereta has all the key elements of Castilian cooking – succulent lamb fed on wild herbs, the smell of smouldering scrub oak, the pungent perfume of paprika, burnt garlic and plenty of olive oil, and, of course, the simplicity of its preparation. With many of the dishes that Pedro had taught me how to prepare it always came back to the same thing. The recipe and the ingredients are neither rich nor complicated, but each dish always has its *punto*. This is what Castilian cooking, at its best, prides itself on. Only practice and experience can guarantee it being *al punto*.

Caldereta is eaten peasant style, where food becomes a communion, straight out of the caldera, accompanied by wine. Bread, cut up into large slabs, is used as a plate and soaks up the juice. The spoons are carved out of horn and oak in the idle hours when the debilitating sun makes it impossible to move on to fresher pastures. Often they are rustic, a pestle at one end with a spoon at the other, sometimes with the addition of a fold-out fork like a primitive Swiss army knife.

'There are always tricks,' said Leandro proudly, 'it all depends on how heavy-handed you are with the paprika. It's never the same twice over.'

After years of outdoor labour Leandro's hands were large and brown, with a hard, smooth skin – not the hands of a three-star Michelin chef. And even the way he handled the knife to chop up the liver was purely practical, lacking anything that might be described as finesse. Now, Leandro cooked caldereta for pleasure. The previous summer, he told me, he had prepared it for 200 people at a local village wedding. He had had ten calderas hanging off their tripods in a long line. Getting them all al punto was nothing short of a miracle and the guests ate everything up. In the past, when food had more to do with survival, more often than not the meat they used was aged mutton; or if one of the lambs fell sick, broke a leg, say, then that would go in the caldera as a treat – a proper peasant dish with no waste. This was how Leandro Martín prepared his version.

1 milk-fed lamb
6 tbsp olive oil
3 cloves garlic
Water
Paprika and salt to taste
1 thick slice fried bread
1 hot red pepper
1 tsp red wine vinegar

In a large, wide pan heat up the olive oil till it begins to smoke, preferably over an open fire. Cut up the lamb into bite-size pieces, reserving the liver, and start to fry. Add garlic and a teaspoon of paprika, and fry until lamb is brown. Cover with water and boil until lamb is tender. Add liver for first half hour then bring it out onto a chopping board. In a pestle and mortar pound the cooked liver, fried bread and hot red pepper into a paste, adding a spoon of water. Add to lamb and season dish with salt and vinegar. Serve.

On my way in to work one morning, I took a diversion up the stairs beside the aqueduct to the Thursday market in the old town. Now that it was getting so hot many of the market shoppers were trying to get in and out by ten. Tomatoes were dropping in price all the time, and the peaches, plums, water melons, small medlars and the two types of cherry, normal and bigarreau, were taking up the space used earlier in the year for cabbages, carrots and the other root vegetables. Salads were wilting in no more than half an hour.

My favourite stall was run by a father-and-daughter team who, unlike the others, sold only home-grown produce. They had a plot of land down near the river, on the fertile banks owned for the most part by the Church. Their choice was naturally limited, but whatever they had was pulled up that morning. I was pleased to see that at last they had given their seal of approval to planting out the vegetable patch. The most superstitious wouldn't put in their tomatoes and garlics until past the night of San Juan. The danger of frost must have passed. The daughter was standing behind her basket displays of baby carrots, the bedding plants and vegetables, and was preparing a few buckets crammed full of freshly cut roses. Down from her were the two potato specialists, a pair of mischievous peasants, one of whom earlier in the winter I saw advertising his produce by eating a potato raw as if it were an apple. The pickle stall was doing well, with its choice of ten different types of olive, and so was the infuriatingly slow lemon, garlic and bay leaf vendor. However many lemons you wanted, one kilo or ten kilos, he would slowly put each lemon in, one painstakingly after the other, and wait for the scales to settle. There was no hurrying him, despite all weighed evidence that there were ten lemons to the kilo. The gypsy clothes stalls had all gone over to summer fashion. The knicker salesman was still working hard. His sales patter was a touch different from most. He would push his hand into the front of a pair of knickers, wiggle it about and shout 'Cover your furries!' It sold the merchandise.

I cut through the backstreets and down towards Duque's. Although there was no reason to fear for my job I still beat Pedro in. Mariano was marshalling the pinches. Thursday was particularly busy in the downstairs bar, so extra trays of tapas had to be made up and little teasers for the grill prepared: slices of marinaded pork, prawns, rashers of cured bacon, stuffed mushrooms and spicy sausages.

All the farmers came in to Segovia to buy and sell cereals, livestock and animal feed. Each of the bars near the aqueduct specialized in one type of produce. It was an animal market, without the animals. So Bar Orly was for sheep, Bar Tropical for pigs, Duque's bottom bar for veal, and so on. The Castilians pride themselves on their honesty and their word being as good as a piece of paper signed by a notario. The truth is that Segovia is so small that reputations are made or broken in one morning, so it doesn't pay to lie or to be too 'sharp-gitana'. If someone sells fifty sheep in good condition, then that's what they are.

The farmers had a healthy appetite. One morning a week, which might be extended to include lunch, they were away from their fields and village. It was a bit of a treat. Coupled with the possibility of making a good deal, bumping into an old friend, there were ample excuses to order that special *ración* – kidneys in sherry, or lamb's sweetbreads.

As the barmen downstairs coped with the influx of customers, the waiters upstairs were preparing the dining rooms for the summer to come. Large blankets were hung up in the doorway to keep out the light and heat, and on all the windows heavy green blinds turned the restaurant into a moonlit world. It took a while for one's eyes to grow accustomed to the new lighting conditions but it was restful. Summer was the period for the siesta and it may have been a gentle way of tricking the body into an early sleep.

Another carnival, this one without masks, was to run from 24 to 29 June. Bands had been booked for the Plaza Mayor every night, and all the barrios had open-air discos and supporting groups. Caché, and Julio and Carmen, had flats on the Plaza Mayor and were dreading the fiesta: five days without sleep. Two you could cope with, but five! Even earplugs didn't work. Julio was half-French, and his more rational side still couldn't understand the Spanish passion for making noise. I sympathized. Often, engaged in a one-to-one conversation in a quiet bar, the other person speaks at a volume which makes you think they think you're half a mile away. It's quite normal for the television and the bar's stereo centre to be on at the same time, competing for limited air space: add twenty voices above that and the repeated horn of a double-parked car to round off a fine auditory cocktail. It's something to do with the fear of appearing dead, or even the fear of death itself, suggested Julio by way of explanation. If a Spaniard isn't blowing on all cylinders he doesn't feel quite right. Noise is a way of proving that you are still very much alive.

A nice idea, said Caché, but he couldn't give tuppence for this form of Spanish expression. He was a *gallego* from the North and his film star dark hair and blue eyes showed his Celtic ancestry. He was from a colder climate. He had two large architectural projects to finish off before the end of the month, so he was moving out to a friend's house tucked away quietly in a dead-end street in the Jewish quarter.

The dawn chorus arrived earlier than expected on the morning of the 24th. At five o'clock I was woken up in our flat by the wailing dulzainas and drums. Three aged women, dressed in black with giant, ornamental hair slides, marched past the balcony. An hour later the first of the fireworks were let off, exploding cannons in the sky. The fiesta had started.

Every day so far the novelty of living in Segovia had filled us with excitement. New sights and sounds attracted us by their hint of the exotic, the weird and the wonderful. There is no denying the Spanish gift for making an occasion memorable. When they go for it they do it with heart. To an outsider it may seem frivolous and shallow but the act of dancing and celebration, even in middle-aged adults, has the urgency and recklessness of teenage abandon. Partying and dancing are hedonistic but not vain and selfish in their obsessive search for pleasure. You dance for others, not just yourself.

On the first night, we danced to the mongrel merengue rhythms from Cuba and Santo Domingo in the Caribbean. On the second, we moved south to the Argentine tango. On the third, it was back up to the Caribbean and the salsa of Ruben Blades. And on the fourth, we danced under the acacia trees to the sound of the Brazilian samba. More than that we couldn't manage. It cost us both in money and health.

Back in the restaurant I was met by tired and sleepy eyes. The fiesta of San Juan and San Pedro had changed the rhythm of life completely. Children of two years and upwards were allowed to stay up well into the early hours and run around the plaza, playing catch round the columns of the town-hall's arcade and dancing with their parents. The next day they would suffer, groan and moan through the morning at school, but a siesta lay ahead. Two days had been made out of one.

The kitchen was now almost as busy at night as it was for lunch. Meals were lighter, but for the chefs it made little difference to the amount of work they had to get through. In some ways, the snacking pattern increased the labour. Instead of a starter and one main course, a whole table of titbits and teasers had to be prepared: chorizos, tortillas, prawns, red peppers, frogs' legs, meatballs, mussels in vinaigrette, roasted quails, marinaded smelts and clams in saffron sauce. And after the shutters had finally been pulled down on the front door, the dirty linen tablecloths and napkins collected and dragged in a sack to the top of the building and the oven scrubbed, Santos, Pototo and Jojo changed into their going-out gear and joined in the fun.

We struggled to keep our eyes open but made it through the dark night of the day on a diet of strong black coffee, aspirins and Vitamin C pills. We could catch up on our sleep in July.

7: Summer and heat

July arrived and summer set in with a vengeance. The heat was debilitating and most of nature went to sleep. The only real activity to be seen was the hectic circling and diving at dusk of the thousands of swifts that picked off the insects. From the balcony the mountains were only just visible through the haze. Day after day was the same, and the weather became closer and more oppressive by the hour. Most of the shopping was over and done with by ten in the morning.

The butcher downstairs was tired and miserable. He lounged against his door and refused to work at more than a snail's pace, regardless of how long the queue.

'It's got to break soon. It can't go on like this.'

Every afternoon purple and angry clouds gathered over the sierra but by nightfall they had melted away. Each day they edged closer to Segovia but couldn't quite make the ten-mile stretch across the lower foothills. On the television the news was repeated with depressing frequency. Forest fires were hitting every area of Spain and decimating hundreds of thousands of acres as they went. The reservoirs were the lowest they had been for a whole decade. If it carried on any longer water would be rationed to a few hours a day. In Segovia the tarmac and stone buildings held the heat all night. The only cool part of the day was at six in the morning just after the lorry that sprayed the streets had passed by. Out in the villages it would be better. The thick walled farmhouses kept out the heat. But the countryside itself had been burnt away. Yellows and browns had replaced the greens of early June. Soon there would be haymaking. One of the few places in Segovia that was now a pleasure to visit was the cathedral, and its museum and the cool of its cloisters.

Exhausted madrileños arrived in Segovia describing their season in hell. The urban jungle the other side of the mountains had hit record highs of 110°F and at night the only place to sleep was out on the balconies, but then you had to cope with the traffic noise and pollution. The only escape was to Segovia, and many fathers had dropped off their families with close relations and battled through the week as best they could de Rodriguez.

In Segovia the siesta was sacrosanct, and respected with complete and utter silence. It was the quietest moment of both day and night. The one group of French students who had walked up the street bouncing the sound from their ghetto-blaster off the walls had met with savage abuse and a bucket of water.

I went down to the butcher and collected a dozen eggs. My appetite for meat had completely disappeared.

'It must break soon. It has to.'

Finally, on 12 July, the purple clouds had moved over Segovia. The tension was almost too much. Hour after hour we waited. The first signs of change were a low and distant rumbling of thunder, and a sudden gust of wind. The first drops of rain fell and teased us with their impotence. But then the lightning released the pressure, which had built up over weeks, like a pin bursting a balloon. What we got resembled a monsoon. The electricity was turned off across the city and the sky lit up. In the flat the rain leaked through in four or five different places, and we rushed around with pots and pans trying to catch it before it went down further and brought down Electric Martín's plaster ceilings. Up in the hills, I was told, the shepherds would be taking shelter by lying down in the middle of their flock away from the trees. Lightning was dangerous. It was an exciting half hour and the air was charged with the strong scent of ozone. The temperature dropped dramatically and life became bearable once again. The electricity came on and we watched the storm moving across the tiled roofs away down the valley.

We walked up to the Plaza Mayor to celebrate with an ice-cold beer. The canopy over one of the terrace bars had been ripped in half by the winds, and billboards, dustbins and road signs had been blown across the street. The storm had blown back some energy into our lives, and the shopkeepers and barmen were rushing round repairing the damage. There were no complaints.

Pedro was back behind the stoves as usual the following day explaining to Fernando's successor how he wanted things done. Manolo had started that morning. He winked at me so often as he strutted round the kitchen, cock of the walk, that I thought he must have a nervous tic. It was just his manner and he was trying to establish communication. Fernando was a hard act to follow; he had been universally popular and there was no side to him. They were as different as chalk and cheese.

'What do you eat at home in this weather?' I asked Pedro.

'I don't, I go home to sleep. My family haven't seen me in months.' He thought I had taken him seriously. 'Hombre, of course I eat something, but I have lost my appetite. I just pick at things. Some sharp Manchego cheese, an anchovy or two, nothing more.'

Incredibly, there were still clients in the restaurant who ordered the hearty roasts. A trip to Segovia was impossible to imagine without tasting its most famous speciality, and perhaps the air-conditioned dining rooms played their part in aiding digestion. The moment they left the restaurant they were hit by a blast of warm wind. No wonder, Cruz told me, that there were so many road accidents in the month of July. Those eaters fell asleep at the wheel.

The one dish that becomes a national favourite during the summer months is the Andalusian gazpacho, and Pedro made gallons of it every morning. There is no strict recipe to follow, everyone makes his own, the way they like it, and even his was never the same two days running. It is a haphazard application of a few basic ingredients and principles. It is better to make far more than you think necessary, because chilled from the fridge it disappears with alarming rapidity. Its consistency is different wherever you go. Some like it as liquid as beer and others with more bite to it so it has to be eaten with a spoon.

1 kg ripe tomatoes
2 slices stale white bread
½ kg peeled cucumbers
4 cloves garlic
Juice of half a lemon
1 tsp cumin seeds
1 large onion, diced
1 green pepper, seeded and diced
4 tbsp virgin olive oil
2 tbsp best sherry vinegar
1 tsp sweet pimentón (optional)
Salt and pepper
Water

An optional selection of favourite fresh herbs which can include: parsley, mint and basil (the herb used by Andalusian lovers to woo and win their beloved)

Soak the bread in the vinegar, oil and lemon juice for an hour. Put everything into a blender and add water to reach the preferred consistency. Stop here to pass everything through a sieve to get rid of the skins, or a mouli legumes if you prefer it to have some body. Chill and serve with a plate which includes finely chopped onion, tiny squares of fried bread, diced green pepper and diced cucumber. People help themselves at table to the garnish.

It is a real reviver and culinary folklore has it that a simple version of it was what every Roman centurion filled his hip flask with when on the march. It seemed quite possible, therefore, that Christ drank from a sponge soaked in this unctuous juice while nailed up on the Cross.

Mariano was filling a gigantic, deep-rimmed paella pan with a selection of vegetables, spare ribs and chicken gizzards, and scooped off all the fat of the bubbling stockpots and added it to the dish. I took out my notebook.

'Can you hang on a moment,' I asked Mariano, 'while I note down the first stage?'

'Of course. More than happy.'

I stood at his side as he threw in stock cubes, vegetable trimmings, an unpeeled onion (presumably for colour), a handful of beef offcuts and some ripe jamón serrano fat. It was stirred around vigorously and then four large bags of rice were added with ample water to cover. As it boiled on a high heat, water was added every few minutes until the dish took on a pudding-like consistency. Mariano scooped out large spoonfuls and put them in plastic containers to store in the cold room. Did I want a taste? It was better cold though, he said. It tasted strong but it wasn't unpleasant, only the texture put me off. The rice was far from fluffy.

I struggled to keep up with Mariano, as he worked so fast. We corrected some of the quantities. What do you call it, Mariano, is it typical of Castile?

'Castile, heavens no. It's a speciality of the house. I don't think they make it in any other restaurant in Segovia. Do they, Pedro?' Pedro nodded in agreement. It was a recipe that had been lost for centuries and recovered only a few years ago by Duque's son, Julián, like his father an amateur food historian. What's it called? I asked again.

'Dog food...' – and Mariano had to lie on the floor, he was laughing so much. Santos barked. They had never heard anything quite so hysterical. Julián had two alsatian guard dogs out on his estate in the country; he was going out that afternoon and needed food for them. They were very spoilt dogs.

I got down to preparing the tapas trays. Maribel, the laundry girl, walked into the kitchen. She was pretty and dark, and would often dress straight out of a fashion page from Vogue – discreet but elegant. She pointed to the tapas tray of stewed tongue.

'Don't eat too much of that, Gisbert. You'll never stop talking. That's what they say around these parts. Too much tongue and you never stop yacking. Haven't you seen how much Big Mouth eats? Why do you think so many people around here have got such good hearing? In winter they get through gallons of the pig's ear stew. Hombre, it makes sense.'

She didn't really believe it but many of the older people in the villages do. It is a hypothesis that is difficult to test out and prove either way; but Castilian folklore still has a strong hold on the imagination of many Segovians. I ought to go out to the villages more often, Pedro told me. That's where the heart of our cooking is.

'Most of us chefs are originally country boys. The latest fashion, of course, is all that over-refined French cooking, but it wouldn't catch on here. The people are too wise to be tricked by that kind of nonsense. What they want is authentic, filling and tasty dishes. There's nothing to beat a cocido, a suckling lamb, or a good potaje, washed down with rosé. And in the summer months, can you think of anything nicer than sitting in the shade of a tree by the river preparing paella? Or barbecued lamb chops?'

It was the month for picnics. Over the last few weekends we had been out to the country whenever possible. Segovia completely changes its character. On Saturday night in the Plaza Mayor I didn't recognize a soul. The madrileños move in because it's cooler than the capital, while Segovians move out to the country because it's cooler than the city. It's good for the catering trade because during the week the restaurants serve their own Segovian customers and at the weekends they fill up again with strangers. Best of all are the foreigners but the busiest month for them had passed. In this heat they were dropping off like flies.

Peli phoned up. Did we want to go up to the mountains for the day and swim? Wonderful idea. We would bring the salad and they would bring the rest. We set off from La Granja and started hiking up the hill. It was going to take a couple of hours to get to Las Calderas – The Cauldrons – but it would be worth the hike. Peli pointed high up the mountain.

'Somewhere up there is the last pair of Imperial eagles. They have nested near to the source of the Eresma. A magnificent bird! This is the most dangerous time for them, what with all the hikers, mountaineers and daytrippers.' We slowly climbed the mountain. Higher up we reached a ravine and crisscrossed from side to side, jumping over the river on the slippery rocks. On both sides of the river the elms had dried up and died, leaving only the waist-high scrub oaks and the sticky lavender bushes. The smell of thyme was overpowering. On the river bank we found the sprouting heads of wild garlic and horseradish. A straggling rosemary bush had fallen on its side with the weight. We scaled a rock and looked down in the direction of Segovia, but the shimmering heat of midday made it impossible to see for more than a few miles. Down below in La Granja the chimney of the Royal Glassworks sent a tower of smoke up from the chimney stacks, which settled above the town on this windstill day. Where we were, the air was noticeably cooler. We arrived at the first of the giant rock pools. Someone else had got there before us. Another twelve to go, said Nievas. It was hard work. Cruz was carrying a heavy basket full of food and wine but she refused to let me take it. An hour later we reached the picnic spot high above the heat haze.

Looking out across the meseta we felt as if we were far out at sea, marooned forever on a rocky desert island. We were all in a poetic mood. I could never get bored of this landscape. After years of living in London it was a joy to rediscover that the horizon line still existed.

We jumped in the ice-cold water and screamed with pleasure, then lay down on the rocks to dry ourselves. Cruz started to unwrap our lunch: pickled olives, giant capers, gherkins, salted almonds, accompanied by anchovies and marinaded smelts as tapas. The smelts and anchovies were laid one on top of the other and skewered with a cocktail stick.

'In Castile they call it a marriage,' explained Peli. 'A sharp and bitter conflict of tastes, the sweet and sour of China. There's nothing better than this to get the salt back in our bodies, washed down with a rosé from Ribera. Heaven!' Cruz unwrapped her silver-foil parcel that contained a tortilla, 'No chorizo, Nieves!' She had left her handbag in the car. Peli pulled out a clasp knife and sliced the garlic carefully over the tomatoes, and from a nearby bush collected a few thyme flowers and crushed them gently over the salad.

We swam after lunch and drove off in the early evening to see the Romanesque church of Sotosalbos on our way home. It is a marvel. The capitals of the portico are carefully worked with sculptures of battling crusaders, castles, condensed Castilian landscapes and medieval country pursuits. The village priest came out of his house and offered to take us on a guided tour. He had single-handedly saved the church from ruin. In one of the chapels he had made a small museum and there we could buy postcards of the church, sculptural details and one of his father's grave. So who was his father? He looked at me slightly nonplussed. What a strange question to ask.

'My father? He was my father. Nobody else.'

The priest led us outside and explained the significance of the sculptures and the particular style of architecture that had been brought back from Syria and adapted to the more pedestrian Romanesque patterns of the North. It was a passionate and informative discourse. It was difficult for him, however, to illustrate his argument with total lucidity without seeing the lunette window at the end of the church. And that was impossible to see without passing through his house into the walled back garden. We followed him obediently. We were a captive audience, trapped in his well-husbanded vegetable patch. The window was nothing out of the ordinary in relation to the rest of the church, but the mere act of seeing it involved a return back through the house. And that's where the business began. Free-range eggs and honey were waiting on the table. Would we like some?

Outside it was beginning to get dark. We left him on the steps of his house with a promise to come back for the concert of Gregorian chant he had organized for Christmas. As we stepped into the dusty village square an enormous combine harvester, called 'The Dominator', rolled towards us with its lights blazing. The farmer was out to start the harvest and was going to work right through the night. They had all been lucky in the country, the storm of a few days ago hadn't damaged the crops;

most of its energy had been expended on Segovia.

Back in Segovia after a long day in the country we went up to the plaza to have the *última copa*. But it was bad form and reckless, said Cruz, to say the última. It was always safer and more realistic to say the penúltima. Segovia was, after all, the city of bars.

I had never been into Bar Jeyma before. It was on the plaza, but I had become a creature of habit and my allegiances were firmly placed with Jai and El Soto. All our friends were there. Occasionally, Julio pointed out, it was worth breaking the mould. I was suffering from Segovia Syndrome, imagining that the universe revolved around La Concha, which has the best tapas. What about José María? Las Columnas? El Ojo?

'So. Where shall we go?' We stood on the street corner discussing the choices. We needed inspiration. It had to be Las Columnas. All I wanted was something simple and clean, a small ración of their juicy and refreshing tuna escabeche. Next stop was Bar Jeyma, on the corner of the plaza. There were only three people standing at the bar but the noise was deafening. It seemed to be coming from out of the woodwork.

The television was up loud but even that was drowned out. I looked above my head and there was a small balcony sheltering the bar. I went up to investigate.

Most of Segovia's female senior citizens, the real decision-makers in the home, were sitting there, gambling for token stakes around the card tables. They were so engrossed they didn't even notice me watching them and they all spoke at once as the bids went flying off the wall. They were the type of women that never waited their turn in the fishmongers and at the market stalls. They were formidable opponents, intimidating and shameless shoppers to a woman. They prodded the produce and demanded the best. In the market they had declared open war. It was up to the stall-holder to try and slip by their guard with a bruised pear, a squashed tomato or a mottled apple, but they were as keen as hawks and the scales always ended up weighed down in their favour. The stall-holders' only weapon against this kind of shopper, the black maids of honour in the Easter procession, was a saucy wit. In the butcher's I overheard one of these hard-headed harridans asking if the steak was tender.

'Tender? How could you possibly doubt it? Tender! My steaks are as tender as the tits of a nun. Excluding the Mother Superior, of course.' She looked appalled and ordered far more than she wanted.

So upstairs at Bar Jeyma was for the old guard. The teenagers, on the other hand, had a whole street to themselves running parallel to calle Réal. During weekends and fiestas it was almost impossible to fight your way through the hundreds of people that spilled out onto the street. The summer months were theirs and seven in the morning was not an unusual time for them to think of going to bed, just as the sun was coming over the peaks of the Guadarrama. The last stop before going to bed was always a churros bar that opened at five to service the late-night revellers. They would have breakfast and then go straight to bed.

On a Saturday or Sunday morning it is never wise to phone a friend before midday at the very earliest unless it is an absolute emergency. I have never got used to it. Some of the most serious funlovers get up for an hour to have lunch and then take a siesta until six. Their body clocks are turned on their heads.

8: Argufying

I had been reading Gerald Brenan's *South from Granada* late into the night because it was too hot to sleep. I stopped at his description of Don Eduardo and thought how little had changed:

> He was a man who liked certainty. His opinions hardened quickly into dogmas because by force of repeating them emphatically he made them true. Thus all contradiction was disturbing to him and the smallest suspicion of doubt opened a gap in that phalanx of solid beliefs which he had assembled for his protection and reassurance. He was ready to fight, therefore, to the last ditch on the most insignificant matters, and when defeated would return to the attack a few minutes later from the same positions.

I had had a similar experience the week before in Bar Prisco. Most of the old boys knew I worked at Duque's and it seemed reasonable to assume that I was a great culinary expert. On questions of food I was therefore the ultimate judge. The old herb collector pushed through the curtains with his walking stick and settled at a table. He saw me standing at the bar and called me over. He opened the plastic bag on the table and spread out hundreds of camomile flowers.

'What do you think these are, then? Any idea?' 'Camomile flowers,' I said. I had seen a family picking them out in the country just a few days before. A small group of men had gathered round to inspect and offer their opinions as well. 'Exactly right!' he said, but he looked annoyed. Where could the conversation go from here? If I had said lime or mint, the argument could have been kept up for half an hour or more. If he didn't think fast he would have to scoop them all carefully back into the bag and his morning's work would have been completely forgotten. 'What if I told you they weren't camomile but they were actually one of the rarer varieties of wild mountain thyme, what would you say then? Do you think it's possible, Miguel?' He turned round to offer his hypothesis to the ex-bullfighter from Cádiz, who massaged it for a few seconds, before offering his reply.

'Anything is possible. You know that.'

If I wasn't going to help the conversation along he would have to take it on himself. He crumbled the flowers through his hand and let them fall on the marble table top.

'If you smell it, you could almost take it for a milder type of thyme. I think that's what it might be. Smell it and tell me what you think.' I put my nose down to the table and it only confirmed my initial opinion. It's definitely camomile, there's no doubt about it, I told him. The matter was closed and I moved back to the bar. 'There is always doubt, you know. How can you ever be absolutely certain about anything? I'm pretty sure now that I made a mistake. I went out this morning to collect camomile and I've come back with a bag of wild thyme. Even the experts can be wrong sometimes.'

The kitchen was in a holiday mood. At the end of the week they were going to celebrate the chefs' fiesta and Clemente was going to take six weeks off.

'I suppose you will be going down to the beach with your family for a few weeks?' I asked him.

'No, not this year. It's become too expensive and anyway in August it's far too crowded. I'll stay home in the village, have a good rest, go out for a few drinks with friends and concentrate on ceramics.' Santos stopped beating the eggs and walked across.

'No, Clemente went to the beach last year and it wasn't a success. On the second day there he ended up in jail.' Clemente tried hard to ignore him. In jail? Whatever for? He didn't strike me as the criminal kind and when I had seen him out at night, or at Fernando's farewell party, he had been almost totally abstemious. 'Yes. Half of his holiday in jail. They won't let him back to Benidorm. It's too dangerous. He's not good for tourism.'

Clemente told Santos not to talk such rubbish. 'It's a sad story, really, it wasn't Clemente's fault. He can't help the way he is. It's the job, you see. Just imagine, Gisbert, if you spent ten hours a day at these ovens basting and turning over the piglets. It would drive you absolutely mad, wouldn't it?' I didn't want to insult Clemente's work because he did it well and it was a skilled job, so that's what I told Santos. Ten hours was a long time and I suppose there was very little variety in what Clemente did. But he was the lynchpin of the kitchen, one of Pedro's right-hand men, and he deserved our respect. 'Clemente just couldn't take it. The change was too much. He's a village boy at heart. You couldn't imagine Clemente at ease in Madrid. Well, Benidorm's not much better. He was like a fish out of water. Totally lost.'

I was fascinated and wondered where all this was leading. Santos continued. 'The problem for Clemente had started on the first day as soon as they had got off the overnight coach. They inspected the beach. His wife and children loved it but Clemente had gone all glassy eyed. They checked in at the hotel but Clemente went straight to bed and refused to come down. He was in a state of shock and needed to rest. A year without a break was a long time.

The next morning he was persuaded down to breakfast but he had completely lost his appetite. Perhaps an hour on the beach and a dip in the sea would be good for him. But he told his wife to take the children on ahead, he might come down later. At midday he slipped on his swimming trunks and stood at the main door of the hotel inspecting the beach. Hundreds and hundreds of sybaritic sunbathers lay spread-eagled out on the luminous golden sands. Clemente's wife spotted him and waved invitingly. Come on down! Clemente waved back but he broke out into a cold sweat, and suddenly felt nauseous and faint. He ran back through the vestibule and up to his room. What was wrong with him? Minutes later the hotel porter tried to stop Clemente as he rushed out of the front door onto the wide, tree-lined esplanade.'

Pedro and Mariano stopped what they were doing, and came across to listen. Santos was an accomplished storyteller and punctuated his delivery with dramatic gestures, facial contortions and colourful turns of phrase. We were all engrossed, except for Clemente, who carried on regardless, occasionally looking at Santos as if to say 'What a jerk'.

'Clemente escaped the clutches of the hotel security staff; dressed in his full chef's uniform with baker's paddle in one hand and a bucket of lard with brush in the other, he rushed headlong onto the beach. The thousands of roasting bodies had only one association in Clemente's brain – cochinillos – and he suffered a short circuit. Down the beach he strolled purposefully inspecting the degree of tanning: a well-bronzed German. He slipped his paddle under the unsuspecting tourist, turned him over and basted him with his brush. His wife was running on behind, screaming for him to stop, but Clemente was possessed. An English couple stood out from the surrounding bodies, red as pan-fried crayfish; succulence itself breathed out of every pore. A quick baste, a squeeze of lemon, a sprinkling of thyme and over went the man on Clemente's paddle. It was done so artfully that the man didn't even wake up; next his wife. Clemente pushed the paddle through under her beach towel, and with incredible ability flicked her over. Out came the basting brush but, horror of horrors, she was topless. The municipal police moved in as his brush went back for seconds.'

Santos had us all in tears. Even Clemente was laughing by the ovens. Santos picked up an imaginary piglet.

'*¡Así y así!* That's how he did it. *¡Así y así!*, like flipping a tortilla. He's a one you know, Gisbert. Keep your eyes on Clemente, he could turn any minute now.'

'How are you coping with the heat?' Pedro asked me. I was beginning to get used to it. After a week of afternoon storms the temperature had fallen noticeably. During the evenings it was even quite fresh, cool enough to wear a jumper. For the last few evenings we had sat out on the plaza watching the violent red sun lighting up the fragile limestone pinnacles of the cathedral before it finally turned to night. The storks were getting ready to leave Segovia before they finally flew off together across the straits to Africa. As many as fifty storks, from all over the province, hovered menacingly high above our heads. They settled on the spires and when there was no more space they rested their stick-like legs for a few seconds on each other's backs. The whole plaza was looking upwards, entranced by the spectacle. Segovia's skyline would be the poorer for it. But they would be back again next January, just in time for the first snows.

Pedro suggested that we should make an *arroz con leche* – rice pudding – together. Chilled in the fridge it is perfect summer food.

1 litre milk	*100 g sugar*
Stick of cinnamon	*Pinch of ground cinnamon*
Piece of lemon zest	*A few tbsp single cream*

250 g Valencian rice

Put the rice in a bowl of cold water, leave to soak for a few minutes, and rinse and wash in a colander. Bring the milk, lemon rind and cinnamon to the boil. Add the rice and sugar, and bring back to the boil. Simmer for half an hour. Allow to cool and put it into the fridge in its serving dish. To serve, stir it around, sprinkle with ground cinnamon and dribble over the single cream.

The prejudice I held against rice pudding had persisted a long time while working at Duque's, but having broken through the barriers of many other taste taboos I eventually gave in. It was refreshing and delicious.

Félix had his day off today but he came into the kitchens anyway. He stood on the waiters' side of the counter for most of the morning swapping stories. Without the companionship of the kitchen he was lost for things to do. All his friends were working here and his village was too far away to waste a day sitting on the bus.

It often happened that most of the younger chefs and pinches would spend part of their free day in the kitchen. Pedro, Mariano and Clemente had the experience of years behind them, and they wouldn't come near the building. They all had their hobbies, and knew the importance of rest and a change. But the younger ones hadn't started their families yet and Duque's was still the centre of their lives. If they went out drinking it was always with other members of the kitchen staff. It may not have come from choice or a love of food but their first marriage was to the restaurant. They were now part of Segovia's catering fraternity and had come to know each other like brothers.

After lunch the restaurant wound down slowly. There was extra cleaning to be done. The next day, for one of the few days in the year, the doors at Duque's would stay shut. It was the chefs' fiesta.

By eleven in the morning most of the chefs and pinches had gathered in their uniforms around the aqueduct. A flat-topped lorry appeared and they all scrambled on. Porrónes of wine and beer were loaded on, and plates of chorizo and ham. The driver set off to the sound of carnival trumpets and traditional Spanish songs. It crawled up the hill to the Plaza Mayor. At the traffic lights they were stopped by the police. Cars behind hooted impatiently, but the chefs danced away on the lorry ignoring them completely. Nothing would stand in the way of their enjoyment, least of all the police who had been bought off with a slug from the porrón and a slice of the best ham. They drove on up to the plaza and accosted the general public whenever they could. Some, like the tiny and ancient Martín, with his permanently weeping eyes, homed in like pigeons. He was eighty years old and still lived in the orphanage; free drinks didn't come his way every day of the year. After a few pulls on the porrón he was persuaded to sing. They all went quiet. Martín's voice was faltering and weak but he gave a soprano rendition of a favourite lovesong. He finished off like a trilling canary, holding his note, and all the chefs clapped loudly and cheered. They banged on the lorry's battered cabin roof.

'Another drink for Martín. *Otro. Otro. Otro. Otro.*' He took a long draught but couldn't be persuaded to serenade them again. The ham was good, though, and so was the chorizo. Was there any bread to go with it? Martín asked. Of course, and Félix cut him a chunk from a giant peasant loaf.

The lorry circled the city until the wine and food ran out. The real fun was about to begin. Down by the aqueduct the mafia of head chefs were building a fire under the direction of the godfather, Tomás Urrialde. They all deferred to his seniority. He looked a splendid figure with his extravagant handlebar moustache and floppy Basque beret. For this one day of the year all his past pupils, Pedro and Pepe Martín included, would serve as his pinches. Pedro was the firewood collector, Pepe Martín was set to chopping the meat and the Parador's head chef teamed up with the chef from José María searching for stones to build the barbecue stand.

The games began. All the restaurants had entered a team for the annual competition. It was a primitive mixture of boules and quoits, played with a small brass plate and rusty old horseshoes. For the last few years Segovia's alternative chefs, who owned their own restaurants but had almost no staff, had teamed up together and swept the board. Flamboyant César, with his floppy chef's toque, and the chef from the Cocina de San Millán, yet again led their team to victory. Their posture and delivery looked suspiciously professional. 'A fix!' cried the Cándido and Duque teams together. And anyway, even if they hadn't cheated by pushing their horse-shoes closer with their foot when no one was looking, they had cheated by practising beforehand. But there was no changing the result. The umpire's decision stood.

Tomás Urrialde was working away. A giant iron cauldron had been lifted onto the flames and litres of olive oil poured in. From the railings above the plaza the chefs' families and friends stood watching the proceedings. Tomás would have to feed 200 or more. It was going to be a caldereta and ten lambs had been cut up into chunks. It was high summer but there was little alternative; a paella for that number of people was next to impossible. They might feed the 5,000 with paella once a year in Madrid and Valencia, but in Segovia it was different. We were in the heart of sheep country. Pedro and Tomás stood side by side browning the meat. Water was thrown in and the stew left to bubble. Was there time for a rematch? No, the teams had lost interest and wandered over to watch Tomás and sample the wine. At last it was ready and the stew served out. All comers received a plate and a cup. And for those who were still hungry Tomás started to barbecue lamb chops, chorizos and thick slices of belly of pork. After lunch, siesta, then off to the bullfight. The restaurants had put up their own *cuadrillas* (the matador and his bullfighting team) but the bulls would be cows. If it was the first fight I was ever going to see, I was warned, it would be better to forget it. It would end in a bloodbath and put me off for life. So the rest of the festivities I left to the chefs.

The following day the spirit of the fiesta had still not worn off. Santos was up to his usual tricks. He pinned down my arm to the worktop and brought down a razorsharp carving knife as if to cut off my hand. At the last second he turned the blade over the heavy weapon brushed my arm with its back. Funny, no? I went to fetch the wine for our lunch. Jojo poured our drinks and disappeared. The kitchen was empty, all except for Pedro. I took a thirst-quenching slurp from the glass and immediately spat it out. It was fiery hot with tabasco and loaded with salt. Out in the hall I could see all the chefs' faces peeping cageily round the door. They exploded into laughter.

Clemente had gone off on his holiday and it looked as if I was going to be his stand-in. Pedro would have none of it. The fiesta was over and from the board it looked as if we would be cooking for two coach parties of Japanese, on top of all the other summer trade. It was time to get down to work and with Clemente's absence the stations would have to be rearranged. Santos and Félix would double up on his job, Manolo and Jojo would fill in their spaces, and Mariano would stay as the roving troubleshooter and whipper-in. It was an important step for Jojo; it meant promotion, something he had hoped for only on his return after a year from the army. Over the last few months his attitude had changed from someone marking time to a serious apprentice chef. He had been caught more than once flicking through one of Pedro's recipe books and had been entered for a local cookery competition. He had become inquisitive, watchful and scrubbed the stove with renewed vigour. With careful nurturing from Pedro he had caught the cookery bug almost without noticing it. It was a just reward for his efforts. If he carried on he might become head chef one day. Pedro put his arm round Jojo's shoulder.

'Don't worry, Jojo, be prepared for mistakes. We all make them. The most important thing is to stay calm and then you will find you always have time to rescue the situation.'

Duque came down into the kitchen. Could Pedro organize another special cochinillo for three o'clock, as there were some politicians coming in? Segovia was a small place and everyone ended up knowing everybody else. In the Sunday evening paseos I was now on nodding terms with almost a thousand people. Duque must have known everyone and everyone certainly knew him. Some afternoons the call-down for special attention became so frequent that almost every client seemed to merit it. We pencilled the clients' occupations on the order chit. It didn't change our lives in the kitchen, we kept on roasting. It would have made twice the work if we cooked to a different standard every time. It was all the same to us: a perfectly cooked cochinillo cost us no extra effort. The only difference was in the final presentation. Did they merit the plate trick or not? Would they get Duque's personalised attentions? But that also depended how many guests there were in the party. The setpiece would obviously lose its dramatic effect on just half a cochinillo.

Sometimes the size of the asparagus served up differed from one to the other. A close friend of Duque's walked in for lunch and all the stops were pulled out with the aim of giving him five-star, ultra-luxury service. A special kilo tin of Avila asparagus was searched for down in the stores. On the side it indicated four to five heads. I opened it and there were only three milky white stems. We laid them out on a plate but they looked obscene, like miniature SS20's. The largest of the three weighed almost a pound on its own. It was garnished liberally with five heaped tablespoons of mayonnaise, the only way of establishing a proper sense of scale.

Jojo had taken to his new position like a duck to water. He had grown in stature and it was now partly his responsibility to make sure that the pinches were doing all that they should. Manolo, the strutting peacock, was winking at me more than ever. I didn't know where to fit into the new arrangement but Pedro kept me firmly under his wing explaining and demonstrating all the different techniques and recipes. He had a horror of my leaving his tutelage without having seen every recipe prepared before my very eyes. In one of the catering magazines he had read a damning report on the new craze of tapas bars in London. It depressed him to think of all the hijacked recipes translated to suit the public's taste. At least the EEC had passed a resolution to allow the export of chorizo and jamón. In Manolo's opinion it was a French and Italian conspiracy because they were frightened of being left with salami and parma ham mountains. But did they really make tortilla using chips? And prawns with garlic, without garlic and the tip of a chilli pepper? I'm afraid they did.

The early morning was one of the pleasantest times to walk around the city. The air was fresh, the shops were closed and there were no cars about. One of the most exhilarating walks was to follow the path out of the walled city that Saint John of the Cross is known to have used when not holed up in his cave. It led under the tower gate of Santiago and down to the barrio San Marcos. Halfway down the slope we spotted our barrio fishmonger cutting down bracken for his window display. We followed the wall round under the Alcázar and the Jewish quarter, and ended up at the bus-station café, one of the few places open for breakfast. On the other side of the road the gypsies were taking a delivery of watermelons from a lorry. They threw them by means of a human chain along the street and placed them carefully inside their green tent that served as a makeshift shop.

The gypsy colony was just up the hill, well out of harm's way, and the new police station was being built next door. The council had supplied them with portakabins but their life seemed to have very little about it that could be described as romantic. If there was a break-in there was little point in asking the average Segovian who it might have been. The gypsies, in the public eye, were always responsible. It was a well-established prejudice in Spanish folklore and Segovia was hardly exceptional in holding onto it.

We dipped our sponge fingers into milky coffee and planned an escape out into the country. West, or east? We never thought about going north out onto the meseta. There was little shade, the rivers had dried out and the villages were mostly ugly stopping-off points after miles of steaming tarmac. Along the edge of the mountains it was different. You could still encounter rivers with water and the villages were relatively cool. In comparison to the meseta people, who hid away all day, the mountain people were dynamic and active. The old ladies sat outside their doors in groups doing crochet, the bars had clients and the farmers could still work out in their fields in the full sunlight.

West would take us into the province of Ávila; east was the picturesque hill-village of Pedraza which Orson Welles had often used as a film set. A friend had joked that it was the only village in Spain where there were more restaurants than inhabitants. If you took away the wild-haired and overweight Argentine (known locally as Pumpkin Pants), as well as the smart Parisian, the English short-story writer and the German pianist, the restaurants outnumbered them twelve to eight. At weekends, we had been warned, it would be like a zoo. Cars queued up to get in through the village gates and then their occupants did the same again to get into one of the twelve restaurants.

9: September

'September is always quiet,' said Pedro. 'All the holidaymakers have returned to Madrid and everyone's spent their money. I'm going to have a few days' break out in the village before the children go back to school. So if you want to go and find some other recipes, now's your chance.' I felt a strong affection and growing admiration for Pedro: for the way he kept control of the kitchen on a hectic August day, his even temper, his generosity and sense of humour. In the mornings he would stand by his locker, change into his working clothes, slip on his clogs and as soon as he entered the kitchen break into a large smile. If he saw me he would shout in his only English, 'One, two, three, Mr Gisbert, very well fandango,' and laugh with pleasure. He deserved a good break. 'Drop in on us in the village if you're passing and come and have lunch, supper, whatever, but it will be my wife's cooking, not mine.'

Whenever I had talked to a chef in another restaurant his eyes would light up when I mentioned Pedro as my teacher.

'A good man. Very honest.'

It was typical of Pedro that he was so open with his recipes. I remember going to one patisserie in Segovia that prepared the special cake, *ponche segoviano*, a delicious mixture of sponge, marzipan and a rich, yolky cream. When I asked the owner if he'd show me how to make it he looked at me in horror, started to twitch nervously and stuttered out his words.

'If I give you the recipe tomorrow, you'll... you'll set up, you'll buy premises opposite here and start selling poncho. No, never. It's a family secret!'

It wasn't Pedro's way, he was eager to help. I looked up the bookings calendar for the coming week and the guide tour groups had fallen right off. I thought I'd take Pedro's advice and use the time to scout around a bit.

Many of the villages had returned to their pre-summer population of around a hundred inhabitants. But near Pedraza, a lot of the sierra villages were celebrating their last fiestas before autumn set in. Bullfights, bull-running, dances in the main village square, fairground stalls, churros stands, barbecues and giant roasts provided the entertainment. Despite all the fun, the shorter days and cooler nights brought on a strong wave of pre-autumn melancholy. We had had the summer; and if there was any truth in the Castilian saying, 'Nine months winter, three months hell', it was due to start snowing within a fortnight.

For us it was the best time for barbecues and paellas cooked outside on the river bank. It wasn't too hot, and the flies and mosquitoes had either died off or were so slow they were easily dealt with. For the Segovians our alfresco eating habits were regarded as vaguely eccentric. Picnics were wonderful. Friends brought tortillas, Segovian Wiener schnitzels, whole rounds of *empanada* – a pastry of tuna, onion and tomato typical of Galicia – and extra bread. We still hadn't learnt to cater for the quantity of bread consumed and it had become a standing joke. Generous friends sometimes brought along a two-foot length of expensive ponche segoviano, which probably cost as much as all the wine and other food put together. Or they brought *suspiros* from Pedraza, a pastry whose name translates as 'sighs', and which is delightfully fragile and light. For one picnic some English friends had stopped off in a village shop and invested in some dubious-looking rosquillas.

Good rosquillas are supposed to stay fresh for six months or more, but nothing deadens the appetite more than having to eat yet another of these cardboard replicas offered and forced onto you by an over-generous hostess. The markets always have biscuit stalls where factory-made produce is sold off cheap, by the weight, and mostly stale. After a string of bad experiences I had given up rosquillas as one of those typical dishes invented by a poverty kitchen with the primary objective of filling the stomach.

Wine was a different matter. My interest in the Castilian grape was growing by the day. José María was the best tutor that one could find. Years back he had become one of Spain's first Master Sommeliers and his passion was for the local wines produced just north of Segovia. Soon, he said, with the profits from the restaurant he would buy his own vineyard and go into production. He checked himself and bent over the table towards me, leaning heavily on both his hands.

'I've already bought one with a partner. It's right in the centre of what we now call the Golden Triangle, within sight of Peñafiel castle. Where could be better? – a few kilometres from Alejandro Fernández at Pesquera and, even further down the valley, there's Vega Sicilia of course.'

His gestures became animated as he started to discourse on his favourite subject with unreserved passion. He had realized a lifelong dream and was rightly proud of his achievement. Sometimes you got the idea that some restaurants could only plan as far as the next meal. José María was quite the opposite.

'It might be as long as ten years before we see any return on our money. Perhaps it will be our sons who will really benefit. Go and see the vineyard if you want, but I must warn you first: the bodega building is still under construction. I'll go and phone Tomás Postigo, the oenologist, now.'

José María left us sitting at the table to sample another glass of his excellent house red, produced by the brothers Pérez Pascuas. If his wine, which they were going to call Pago de Carraovejas, lived up to his expectations, then by 1995 his first *crianzas* – oak-aged wines – and reservas would put him firmly on Spain's wine map as one of the prestige bodegas.

José María strode back across the dining room to our table.

'Tomorrow, if you can make it, Tomás Postigo will be waiting for you at three o'clock in Bar Peñafiel on the Valladolid crossroads. I can tell you more about the vineyard but I'd rather leave it to the real expert. I only beg of you one thing, please overlook the building works.'

The next day I drove up across the meseta to Peñafiel. There was not a vineyard to be seen. Then, suddenly, a few kilometres before Peñafiel, the ground dropped away dramatically into the wide valley through which the Duero river meandered peacefully, irrigating the valuable wine crop.

Tomás walked up the slope, stopping occasionally to give the vines a quick inspection. He teased a vineleaf between his fingers as he surveyed the slopes. Each vine had its individual water source and was carefully trained along a wire. They were maturing well. Most of the vines were now between three and four years old, and with careful pruning they were ready for the first test harvest. The inspector from the Ribera de Duero *denominación de origen* pulled up in his car. He was as fascinated as I was with Tomás's explanation of the bodega's installation. Over the last few years Tomás had travelled all over Spain and Bordeaux carefully selecting the perfect marriage between state-of-the-art technology and the most traditional methods. His small team of pickers was already out in the field carefully laying the grapes in trays no deeper than a shoebox. Many bodegas used a pump system to pull the grapes up into the giant steel vats but Tomás felt that this inflicted excessive stress on his valuable grapes. It would be an excellent wine, I suggested to him. And he laughed as he interjected: 'It better be, or else José María will kill me.' I reported back to José María the following day and he was happy with my first impressions.

He then suggested I visit the Pérez Pascuas themselves, or the Protos cooperative at Peñafiel, or Pesquera, or even the legendary Vega Sicilia vineyards a few miles down the road. The latter would be difficult, it would need a phone call. Better still visit them all. I might be lucky and be asked to stay for lunch. There was nothing to beat a full-bodied Ribera red, sipped slowly, and accompanied by milk-fed lamb chops barbecued slowly over the embers of last year's vine shoots. Now was the time, he told me. The grape harvest was just days away.

I drove north out of Segovia and followed the road to Aranda de Duero. Out on the meseta the farmers were burning back the stubble. Fires lined the horizon and the smoke rose slowly over the open plains. I stopped at Fuentidueña for my mid-morning snack. The village was now almost in ruins, but once it must have been magnificent. Back in the sixties an American had passed by and bought one of the Romanesque churches, shipping it back to New York stone by stone, where it now sits in the Metropolitan. The woman behind the bar became passionate.

'The Yankees want everything. They bought it for next to nothing. Then, of course, $1,500 seemed a king's ransom. And now they say it's caught a mould with the damp sea air and the stones are disintegrating. Turning to powder! Aagh, those Yankees!'

From Fuentidueña I drove straight to Vega Sicilia. The phone call had been made and Don Mariano, the chief oenologist, was waiting on the steps of the old red-brick bodega. He had been born on the estate, the son of a farmhand, but the previous owner had spotted his interest and sent him to train first in Madrid and then in Bordeaux. It was an ironic twist, because most of the bodegas of the area, as in La Rioja, had been founded by the Bordelais at the end of the last century after the phylloxera disease had destroyed their own crops.

Don Mariano was excited. The harvest was near. It might even start at the weekend. He ran across the gravel forecourt.

'Come, we'll just have a check.' Out of his pocket he pulled a tiny pestle and mortar, and a device for divining the alcohol content. He pulled a few grapes off the vine and vigorously mashed them up. 'These tempranillo grapes form the base of our fame. We use other varieties, of course, like Malbec and Merlot, to name only two, but it's the tempranillo that is the jewel of Castile. It's that and a hundred other variables that give Vega Sicilia its unique character.' He poured the crystal-clear liquid into the device and held it up to the sun. He beckoned me over. 'It's as I thought: 12.5 degrees. If it goes on like this then we're only three days away.'

Vega Sicilia is a wine veiled in mystery and the rumours abound. Winston Churchill had loved this fine little claret. So, apparently, does Prince Charles. He felt it would serve well at his wedding reception. The diplomatic channels were tapped but not a drop was forthcoming. Perhaps they could pull a few strings through family connections. Don Juan Carlos, King of Spain, was requested to intervene. The reply came back fast. Just this once, they would make an exception. But they could only permit two cases, no more. I asked Don Mariano if the story was true. He didn't know. It might be, but probably not.

'Hombre, El Rey is El Rey and Prince Charles was a very lucky man.' For Lady Di, the darling of the Spanish press, I think they would have sold the vineyard. 'What is absolutely true is that the only bottle that has ever been given away free was a few years ago, to the Pope. The label is framed, up in the bodega office.'

The kudos of Vega Sicilia is powerful indeed. The only way to acquire the wine is to join the buyers' list. The waiting list now runs to twenty years. Once you are on, you can start with a small purchase of a couple of bottles, building up your quota bit by bit over the years. There are three sins that you can commit to be struck off the list: if you don't order for two consecutive years, in which case you are probably dead or bankrupt; if you are difficult about payment; or if you deal on the black market. The last is easy to discover, as every bottle is numbered and they know who owns them all. Two years ago a rakish señorito had paid for a luxury holiday in Marbella by selling off his stock at a fabulous profit. He wouldn't get another bottle again. Such was the mystique that one wine shop in Madrid lost all its stock when an inattentive assistant sold all in one go. The owners panicked. How could you possibly be considered a serious vintner without Vega Sicilia? By the afternoon they had traced the owner and offered him double the price he had paid. No, treble! By eight o'clock that evening the wine was back on the shelf – and at the same price as before.

Don Mariano wasn't interested in the stories, they went way over his head. He lived and breathed the wine, and as we stepped into the bodega, what a smell! We would start at the beginning. That morning they had already picked a test load which might, or might not, be used as the 'foot'. The 'foot' – the early test crop – would be allowed to ferment a few days before the proper harvest and divided up between the giant stainless steel vats. It would give the rest of the grapes a kick-start. After a few months the wine would be put into oak barrels and that's when the real fine tuning would begin. Put first into an aggressive American oak, it would then be filtered over to a French oak a few years later for its rounding out. The earliest any Vega Sicilia 'Unico' is released is after ten years but there are some still ageing slowly in barrels from the 1960's.

Mariano tapped the bung out of a barrel and lowered in a glass pipette to draw out the wine.

'You and I are the first ever to taste this wine.' It was from last year's crop and he was giving it a routine check to see how it was going. 'The earliest this one will be on the shelves is the year 2000.' He slurped again. 'But I have my suspicions about it; it could reach reserva status, in which case it might be as late as 2010.' I wondered how Mariano managed to contain his energy and obsessive interest given the excruciating patience required to produce the wine. We walked into another large barrel-lined hall where Mariano tapped another bung. The pipette was lowered in. 'Can you remember that tannic taste? It ought to have reduced with this wine.' We looked at the colour, holding up the glass to the light. Mariano's tasting techniques were infectious, and as his conversation was almost completely devoid of the recherché terminology of winespeak, I felt I was beginning to learn. There were no hints of raspberry, vanilla, tobacco or gooseberry flavour to identify. At my stage, as a total beginner, the only important thing was to drink seriously, and compare and contrast. Enjoy it, he said, the rest of the nonsense could come later if I wanted. We proceeded from barrel to barrel and Mariano was obviously noting everything down in the complicated catalogue of tastes he held in his memory. I was certainly enjoying it and was becoming lightheaded. 'It's a funny thing but the previous owner, a Hungarian refugee, didn't really understand what he was sitting on here at Vega Sicilia. He bought the estate because he liked the house and it was convenient for his summer holidays. He drank the wine like a table wine. It wasn't special to him but he loved every drop.'

Mariano advised me to try the other wines of the area. There was no competition between them because they all had a different house style. 'Unico', as its name suggested, is a lone star. Nothing could ever be passed off for it.

The bodega at Pesquera, owned by Alejandro Fernández, is a different story altogether. Compared to Vega Sicilia it is a humble cottage industry. The advantage it holds over Vega Sicilia is that you can buy the wine over the counter and enjoy it later in the quiet of your home. Until a few years ago it was completely unknown.

An American wine writer was doing his duty calls of the area. Alejandro opened a run-of-the-mill bottle for him and he thought it good, very good indeed. They worked back through the vintages and it knocked the connoisseur's socks off. He hadn't expected anything worth buying but he had to eat his hat. Alejandro took me into his office where he cut off slices of a mature Manchego. We walked across the courtyard and into the bodega. Between all the different tastings we nibbled on the cheese.

'Did you see the building site as you crossed the river by the bridge? Well, with the good fortune I've had, thanks be to God, I'm building a wine museum of the area. We stepped our quality up as soon as we discovered the sophisticated French techniques, and a lot of the old machinery and methodology became redundant. The old-style wines were far too strong, but that was how the villagers liked it. One day, I might try to make a batch of that type again, just a little, to see how it really compared.'

Alejandro was as obsessive as Mariano; they were both slaves to the grape. He apologised that he hadn't got a good Jabugo ham to help down the wine but I didn't feel it needed much assistance. It was fortunate that the threat of the breathalyser, like so many things in Castile, was still no more than notional. In Segovia, there was in fact nothing abnormal about seeing a policeman on duty breaking the boredom of his routine with a large measure of brandy, or a *sol y sombra* – sun and shade – a fifty-fifty mix of brandy and aguardiente. But that was only in the mornings.

I had had enough wine tasting for a day. I had only been to two bodegas, and I still had to taste the rosés, the whites and the peculiar *palo cortado* – a Castilian sherry.

September is the month for pelota matches and the suicidal ritual of the bull-running. In some areas of the province there is never a day when one of the neighbouring villages isn't celebrating some saint's day or other. For the shepherds and farmers the month is one long non-stop party.

The pelota competitions are held in every single village. It's a primitive form of squash played in pairs but the Castilians had added a further macho element to the long and exhausting game. In the Basque country, a few hundred miles north, it's played with baskets strapped to the arm and in other parts of Spain wooden paddles are used instead. In Castile, the ball, harder than a tennis ball, is hit directly with the bare hand. The victors of the knockout competitions have red and swollen hands, and one friend claimed that when his father got home after a match his mother used to stand on his to stop the swelling. Bandaging for protection is regarded as bad form. The whole village comes to watch and stay on for the prize-giving of legs of wind-dried ham.

It's exciting but not as exciting as the bull-running. The walled village of Pedraza has the most picturesque run in the province. After a long night of non-stop drinking the young men of the village dust themselves down and get ready for the climax of the night's activity. The crowds climb up on the high barriers that line the steep road and look out across the plains. On the occasion we went, we waited impatiently for an hour. Where were the bulls? And suddenly the atmosphere became electric as a cloud of dust rose up from over one of the hills. Everyone readjusted their positions on the barriers, making sure they had a firm and secure foothold. To fall could mean death.

The bulls appeared in the distance trotting slowly towards us. Behind them twenty horsemen with long wooden lances corralled them in our direction. They were still half a mile away but the adrenalin pumped fast. As the bulls hit the road at the bottom of the hill they picked up speed. The first of the boys jumped off the barriers and goaded the bulls with their red handkerchiefs. The bulls slowed down as they saw the assembled crowd but then put on a dramatic burst of speed as they picked out the runners. The crowd went wild as groups of runners threw themselves on the ground to avoid the lunging horns. They had rounded the hairpin safely and were now making up the hill towards us. They were tiring and slowing down, and that, my neighbour on the fence said, was when things got dangerous.

They stopped completely and the bravest of the village youths ran down to meet them and poked the animals' noses with rolled-up newspapers. They refused to respond. And then, just at the moment when all seemed lost, the largest of the bulls lifted its head and charged at our fence. My heart leapt into my mouth as I could feel the fence giving. The cross-beam splintered and we fell down ten feet. There was total chaos but nobody was hurt. My neighbour on the fence lifted me out of the wreckage and suggested the only sensible cure was to retire to a bar and calm the nerves with a brandy. Afterwards we should come back to their village and share their lunch. Fate had brought us together with Paco and María del Mar, an eccentric and strange-looking couple.

He was lanky and could in his youth have appeared handsome, but his face had been transformed by the sun into a deeply lined leather mask, burnt almost black. His hair stuck out from the back of his head like a shelf. His face cracked into a large smile. We had been lucky, hadn't we? María del Mar giggled nervously in agreement. It was too much excitement for one day but even so they might come back again tomorrow at the same time. They loved the bull-running. Paco used to run himself in his youth but stopped after a goring. He pulled up his trouser leg and displayed a deep gash that had been stitched together clumsily and had folded the flesh double into a ghastly crimson crevice. This kind of wound was nothing nowadays, said María del Mar. With the main road to Segovia ready and the advent of the motorcar, you could be on the operating table at the general hospital in half an hour. Poor Paco had had to perform his own operation with the help of another friend and the next morning he took the village bus into Segovia. It had gone septic and he had missed two weeks' work. It was terrible that, missing two weeks' work. He hadn't missed a day before or since. A shameful episode.

We followed their second-hand hearse back to their village forty miles in the wrong direction. The house was a large farmhouse on the outskirts of the village, with a room for the dogs, one for the pig and another for the chickens. Upstairs in the attic a plague of rabbits was breeding away happily. They were a good source of protein and particularly tasty in paella. María del Mar asked if we wanted her to kill one now but we declined the offer. She did it anyway and passed me the animal.

'You'll enjoy it tonight in Segovia.'

Paco hauled a case of beer bottles out of the cellar and ordered us to sit down at table. Lunch wouldn't be long, it had been bubbling away in the open fire for all morning. It was a stew, but when I put my spoon into the glutinous mess it defied description. It was like nothing I had seen in Duque's. It was excellent for keeping out the cold that blew off the mountains, explained Paco. Before I had got the third spoonful down María del Mar had filled the empty space on the plate with another ladleful. The dish was an adaptation of a recipe of her mother's who had died when María del Mar was eight. It included tripe, pig's heart and lungs.

We left Paco asleep at the table and María del Mar came out to the gate with us. 'We could have a chicken as well, if we wanted.' No, the rabbit was quite enough for just the two of us, thank you.

10: Cocido

Our half Polish-half Spanish doctor friend Orsi told me that he and his fellow lunch-club members had finally, at the end of a long and tough season, reached a unanimous decision as to who made the best *cocido* in the province of Segovia. It is a serious matter and definitely not to be repeated within earshot of madrileños. Moves were made earlier this century to proclaim cocido the national dish of Spain but Madrid jealously claimed it as its own. All other versions are branches off the same tree. Still, the unofficial winner of the cocido castellano competition this time round was Nicolás, the chef at La Concepción bar in the Plaza Mayor. The one person Orsi's friends hadn't thought of telling was Nicolás himself. So when I told him why I wanted him to teach me how to prepare this dish, he was only too happy.

Its typical Segovian flavour, he explained, arose from various factors. There was almost an infinite number of possibilities and variables. He used bay leaf but no morcilla. He put in carrots but left out leeks and always used the best quality extra-virgin olive oil. The chickpeas were a local variety. The chorizos came from a nearby town, Cantimpalos, specializing in their production. He liked to be a little bit more generous than the average frugal housewife when he put in the knuckle of a wind-dried jamón serrano. With more than a dozen varieties of chickpea, twenty styles of morcilla and fifty types of chorizo available, any variation in these alone would noticeably change the final result. And then of course there was the quality of the local bottled mountain water. It's on the subject of drinking water that a Spanish gastronome can really go to town. I haven't visited a single village in Castile that doesn't have better water than the neighbouring village – 'probably the freshest and cleanest water in the province', and, some have even said, 'the best water in the whole of Spain'. The Iberian Peninsula. Europe. The world. In a hot and arid climate there is always a premium put on a good, reliable water supply. I remember talking to one homesick Galician – Galicians are famed for homesickness – who brought bottled water back to Segovia from his village in the North, not to drink, but to put in a stew.

Cocido, however, is not just a dish but an authentic ritual. In the last century in Madrid's boarding houses, cocido was served every day of the year except during Lent. It is really a three-course meal in one. First comes the soup, then the vegetables, and finally the choice of meats and sausages. Of all the great winter dishes Spanish cocido is one of the best. The smell of it bubbling away for hours on the stove is reason enough not to mind that summer has ended and autumn arrived.

Apart from the glorious taste and smell it's also wonderful to be eating your way through the annals of Spanish history. The essential ingredient in cocido, the chickpea, came into Spain with the Carthaginians between 800 and 500 BC. The dish, or a close cousin, then appeared with the *adafina* or *dfeena*, of the Sephardic Jewish community. Also from the Arabic word *defano*, meaning to cover, the dish can automatically be related to two-thirds of Segovia's populace in the early Middle Ages: the Jews and the Moors. The next significant progression was the addition of the pork products, particularly that of *morcilla* – a blood sausage, or black pudding – which insulted and doubly transgressed two of the essential tenets of kosher preparation and the Jewish dietary code. After 1492 and the expulsion of the Jews, eating cocido was an even finer test than the cochinillo lie detector for the authenticity of the conversos' change of faith. More than a century later, the New World tuber – the potato – was added and possibly around the same time in the Spanish court pasta, or fine noodles, found their way into the soup. It also appeared in these years as the *olla podrida*, a dish that Sancho Panza forbids the starving and idiotically gullible Don Quixote to eat.

There was no holding back in La Concepción's upstairs kitchen. Javier, Leandro and Juan Jo, the waiters on the early shift, who must have eaten the dish hundreds of times, were waiting eagerly and telling Nicolás to get a move on. The stockpot had been on the go for over four hours.

For the preparation of Nicolás's cocido castellano the long list of ingredients may seem off-putting, but cooked once it becomes obvious that it is a dish that looks after itself.

5 litres water
soaked overnight
200 g belly of pork (tocino)
2 tbsp olive oil
200 g fresh chorizo (not dried)
200 g beef bones
½ kg shank of beef in one piece
200 g serrano ham bone with marrow and some ham
1 whole head of garlic
4 medium-sized carrots
1 large onion, skinned but whole
2 bay leaves
½ kg chickpeas, soaked overnight
½ kg pre-boiled cabbage
4 cloves garlic, sliced
Vermicelli

For the pelotas (dumplings):
1 egg
1 tbsp chopped parsley
2 tbsp finely diced belly of pork from pot
2 tbsp finely diced chorizo from pot
Half glass of dry white wine
Salt and pepper
Breadcrumbs to make paste

In a large stockpot – which will eventually hold all the ingredients – put the water and all the meats, head of garlic, onion and bayleaves. Bring to the boil and simmer for an hour, skimming occasionally. Add the soaked chickpeas and continue to simmer for a further two and a half hours. Quarter the potatoes and halve the carrots, and simmer for a further half hour.

At this stage you will have time to make the pelotas, although they are optional. Lift the chorizo and belly of pork out of the pot and cut off enough for two finely chopped tablespoons of each. Replace the rest. Put the finely diced meats and the other ingredients, except for the breadcrumbs, in a mixing bowl, and stir into each other. Slowly add the breadcrumbs until you have a firm but distinctly moist paste.

Use two tablespoons to form balls, fry them until golden, then lower them gently into the stockpot. Now you can season the cocido with salt – not before, as it might prevent the chickpeas from becoming tender.

When the carrots and potatoes have had their half hour, strain off enough stock for the required number of bowls of soup. Heat up in another pan with the vermicelli until tender and serve as the first course.

Heat some oil and fry the garlic cloves until golden brown but not burnt, throw in the cabbage and heat through, stirring rapidly. Put the cabbage on a serving dish and surround it with the other vegetables, the chickpeas and the pelotas, trying to keep them as separate from each other as possible so that it doesn't resemble a mixed salad. Serve.

Turn off the heat, and when the vegetables have been eaten cut up the meats and serve.

Another wonderful everyday dish that can easily become addictive is *lentejas* – lentil stew. Again, as with cocido, the magical taste of lentejas comes from the paprika-laden chorizo which combines so well with the earthiness of the lentils. A dribble of good vinegar and extra-virgin olive oil is sometimes added at the end.

There was no difference between the digestive systems of the other chefs and myself, so it suited us all to ration the lentils to a couple of days a week at the most. Whenever we had them we ate too much. It reminded me of a passage in Maura Laverty's autobiographical reminiscences of Spain, *No More Than Human*, which puts the lentil, poor man's food, into its proper Spanish historical context:

> A diet of bread and lentils fills you with wind. There was a loud noise as a million half-starved Spaniards relieved their flatulence. The noise was heard in the Royal Palace in Madrid. It sent the heart of King Alfonso into his mouth.
>
> 'Is it the legs of my throne I hear cracking?' he asked.
>
> 'No fear of that, your Majesty,' Primo de Rivera assured him. 'Didn't I put grand new legs under your throne with my own two hands? The noise you're after hearing was only your loyal friend and subject, the Marques de la Rojas, clipping the end off his cigar.'
>
> '*Esta bien*,' said the King, and he relaxed. But he knew, and Primo de Rivera knew, that the noise had a threat in it.

In the Hunger Years, when apparently not a cat or dog was to be found outside the stockpot in Madrid, lentils were eaten almost every day. Even nowadays the butcher is reputed to leave the heads on the rabbits just so you can see what you're getting.

At La Concepción, where Nicolás prepares as good a lentil stew as you'll get anywhere, Jai, the owner, has sorted out a way of serving it to avoid all the digestive-related problems. In October, for the first time, the refreshing, iced bowls of gazpacho are put away, to be replaced by something heartier. Out come the stews. The steaming lentils rest in their polished copper pan and are kept warm by a spirit lamp on the bar top.

The serving of them has as much to do with etiquette as it does with Jai's whimsy. They are almost never served with the first drink, and often not with the second, regardless of how bitterly cold it is. Perhaps with the third, Jai will reach over and spoon some of the stew into a small, individual, brown china bowl and send it down to your end of the bar. You have to earn the tasty reviver which, as you don't pay any more for it, is really a gift. One way is through friendship and the other is by drinking a lot. In the end, the two amount to about the same thing. The lentils, however, are served in just the right quantity, just enough to stave off hunger and keep out the cold – the perfect tapas to excite the tastebuds and set your thoughts on lunch.

Then there is the great bean dish. In the opinion of many Segovians the only place to eat judiones de la Granja is in San Ildefonso de la Granja itself. Situated just outside Segovia, the town surrounds the imposing palace of the Bourbon kings, a monument to French Classical style. There is nothing French, however, about a steaming plate of judiones. It is probably the heaviest of all the Castilian dishes and its restorative properties are such that it used to be fed to the shepherds during the exhausting sheep-shearing days to keep up their strength. After six months of working with Pedro I finally overcame the horror of that first job he gave me: the scorching of the pigs' trotters, ears and cheeks. It was now cold and wintry, so I tried the dish. It was honest and good, and the large butter beans were creamy and soft. It wasn't for every day but after a long hike up the mountains behind La Granja during the winter, it would be the right thing to have on return.

The butter beans are grown in town. Down below the palace and the polo pitch, the allotments start. They are owned by the Patrimonio Nacional, Spain's equivalent of English Heritage, and divided up equally between families who reside and pay their taxes in the town. In autumn the area is a jungle of bamboo beanpoles. Few of the families harvest more than their immediate needs, but if they do they sell them straight to the restaurants, of which Dolar is reputed to be the best. It is a good cash crop and the market gardeners expect to get 1,000 pesetas a kilo for their luxury item. The beans then double in weight after an overnight soak.

Judiones de la Granja is a long time in the making but keeps improving over a period of four days. It is one of the reasons for its popularity during shearing time, the busiest days of the farming calendar, when cooking time is at a premium. Giant cauldrons are prepared in advance and the only job left is to reheat them.

It was at Dolar that the matriarchal figure of Teresa, Javier El Soto's mother-in-law, took me under her wing. She was one of those rare examples of a professional woman chef, and took great pleasure in passing onto me all the tricks and special techniques needed to succeed in producing this local masterpiece. The best months for making it, she told me, were October and November, when the judiones were still only semi-dried and the appetite for the dish was not yet jaded.

Teresa observed some very strict rituals when she was making the dish. The finished item was always left to rest again overnight. It was then that it did most of its cooking. Somehow, the magical butter beans would soften and thicken the sauce like a mayonnaise. The dish was always left to cool in the very same pot. Hot was never mixed with cold leftovers and she even went to the length of washing the wooden spoon every time after she had stirred the pot. If she forgot to do this or by oversight mixed up different pots a chemical reaction would set in and the dish was doomed to failure. When cooking for the public it was important to take extra care.

½kg dried butter beans
100 g belly of pork
1 bay leaf
1 head of garlic
1 pig's ear
1 pig's trotter
1 morcilla sausage
Water
1 tbsp sweet pimentón
2 tbsp olive oil
1 onion, finely chopped
1 tbsp flour
1 chorizo sausage

Soak the beans in water for at least twelve hours. Drain, pick over and wash. Put the beans in a pressure cooker, along with the belly of pork, bay leaf, garlic head, chorizo, and pig's trotter and ear, cover with water and cook for an hour. If not using a pressure cooker simmer for three hours. (The pressure cooker may seem like cheating, but it is in fact an improvement, as the butter beans move around less and lose the tendency to disintegrate.) Take out the garlic and bay leaf, and discard. Put the belly of pork, trotter, ear and chorizo to one side. Fry the onion in olive oil until transparent. Stir in the flour and pimentón, and add to the beans. Add a glass or two more of water and simmer for a further twenty minutes. Add salt to taste. In a separate pan of water poach the morcilla for twenty minutes. Allow everything to cool until the following day. Take off some of the stock from the beans and warm the chopped-up meats in a separate pan. Heat the beans through thoroughly. Serve the beans in individual heated bowls and garnish with the meats. Serve.

Back at Duque's, it was strange to return to the rigid restaurant hierarchy after a weekend with Teresa. She had her assistant but the relationship between her, the rest of the family who ran the front of the shop and the clients was a different culture from the regimentation at Duque's. In the kitchen Pedro and Mariano were as amiable and approachable as ever but the waiters lived in their world, the washer-uppers in theirs; Maribel lived on her own in her ivory white tower of tablecloths and napkins, the accountants and bookkeepers hid away in their office, and the Duques stayed above it all concentrating on customer relations. It had to be that way, but I thought if you had to sacrifice your life to the stoves then Teresa was a woman blessed.

There weren't many of her kind left in Segovia; and although her authentic *cuisine grand-mère* was coming back into vogue in the cookery magazines and restaurants, they seemed to forget that the most vital ingredient was Grandma herself. Her character pervaded the restaurant, as it did in Bar Zaca in La Granja and the Venta Pinillos in Polendos. Comfort and familiarity put you at your ease straight away. A bottle of house wine and a loaf of bread were put on the table while you waited, and already they had you won over with the quirky decoration and the bare necessities of survival. Children were a different story altogether. Even the cooking was put aside for a few minutes. Food was important, but not so important that it couldn't wait while Grandma got to know her next generation of clients. It was life, not food, that mattered most.

11: A Fight

Manolo had found it difficult to integrate. He had come in to replace Félix who had moved across to the kitchens of José María. In many ways Pedro was right when he said we were all in a culinary kindergarten. For me, the experience had been like going back to primary school, or the Boy Scouts, with the same jealousies, rivalries and strong friendships. There were the same rules, accepted codes of behaviour and the highly structured pecking order. Commands were given and had to be accepted. Duque was chairman of the board, paymaster and headmaster all rolled into one. He was necessarily distant. But it fell to Pedro to be available for counselling, hand out advice and offer encouragement. He was kind by nature and authoritarian by training, a mentor and father figure to them all. He gave Manolo short shrift.

'Maybe in the restaurant in Valladolid you did things like that but this is how we do things here. You do it because I say so.' Manolo became prickly and resentful, and would walk off.

Manolo had worked for five years in the Valladolid restaurant, so technically he knew the ropes. But he desperately wanted to break into the small circle of intimacy that had built up over the years between Santos, Clemente, Mariano and the other pinches; they resisted his blundering offers of friendship. He didn't know exactly where he fitted. He had come in as an assistant chef above the pinches and it was essential he proved his worth. The pinches resented him. He was too cocky and laddish, and when everyone laughed he laughed the loudest. I felt sorry for him. For me the settling-in period had been difficult but completely different. Everyone had put themselves out and wanted to play a part in my education. They were proud of their beautiful city and the delights of its cuisine, and wanted to share it with me. Manolo, from the neighbouring province of Valladolid, would have his own opinions and doubts about the relative merits of Segovia; and as every Segovian knows, there's just no competition. Manolo had lost before he had even started.

There was going to be a buffet for local government officials in La Floresta and Manolo was ordered to cut the bread into triangles for the canapés. Mariano showed him how. Manolo had his own views on the subject. Mariano walked over to him and again demonstrated the exact technique required.

'They are for canapés, Manolo. We're not making two thousand cheese sandwiches. Just do it as I say, all right?' It was obvious by now that Manolo was intent on making his point; the spark of rebellion had fired up in him; he was going to stand his ground. Mariano looked across the kitchen and studied Manolo carefully. He strode over once more and threw Manolo's wasted efforts into the bin.

'Have you got some kind of problem, Manolo? Do you want me to show you again how to cut a piece of bread into four triangles? I could get any of the waiters in here and they would make a better job of it. Look, arsehole, I'm not asking you to prepare a fucking soufflé!' Mariano was fuming. I had never seen him so before. We had all managed to pass through the exhausting Easter period and the hellish summer months without anyone losing their temper. However irritable we'd been, we always treated each other with a certain degree of respect. We were all in the same boat, after all. Mariano raised his voice. 'Do you think it's normal that I should have to waste my time showing some dickhead of an assistant three times how to do the simplest of jobs? I can't see the point of teaching you anything. You obviously know how to cook better than Pedro and I, so why don't you go upstairs to Duque and offer to take our jobs? I'm sure he'll jump at the chance.'

Dominga, Rellés and the other washer-uppers crossed the landing to see what the commotion was about. Waiters came running into the kitchen. It was too good an opportunity to miss. Manolo was at the point of no return. He would have to go through with it now, to the bitter end. He couldn't afford to lose face in front of his new kitchen companions.

It was beginning to look very ugly. He backed away from the work surface with the razor-sharp carving knife gripped tightly in his outstretched hand. Pedro came rushing up from the cold store. With his free hand Manolo cupped his genitals. An animal scream exploded from his mouth.

'Cuckold! You son of a whore! You've touched my eggs!' He gesticulated demonstratively with his manhood. 'You've touched my eggs!' he screamed again. It was a total loss of pride and I had read enough about the explosive Latin temperament to fear the worst. His eyes fixed on Mariano with an unforgiving hate.

Manolo threw the knife across the kitchen and it smashed against the metal work surface, bouncing to the floor. He moved towards Mariano, who stood his ground firmly. With one sweep of his arm Manolo smashed an earthenware crock full of judiones to the floor. Pedro moved towards him.

'¡Basta! ¡Basta! I leave you alone for five minutes and I come to find this. Manolo!' The unequivocal tone in his voice brooked no argument. 'You will sweep up that mess immediately. And you will never ever throw a knife in my kitchen, do you hear? Not if you have any intention of keeping your job.'

With his tail between his legs Manolo picked up the brush. The confrontation had fizzled out as fast as it had started. His explosive display of temper was no more than theatre and his pride had just about been salvaged from the wreckage of his first few weeks in Duque's kitchen. In the future it would make a good story. And minutes later, it had been transformed into an epic drama, with both he and Mariano acting out their dramatic roles for those who hadn't had the good fortune to be present. Manolo had found his place.

One of the mushroom collectors came into the kitchen during the afternoon with two heavily laden plastic bags. He hadn't been seen since spring, but it had rained on and off for the last two weeks and the autumn crop was ready for picking. He opened them out on the bench and Pedro inspected them thoroughly, throwing away a few insects that had travelled in with them.

'They're all right. Nothing special, though. How much do you want for them? I couldn't use the smaller ones for anything else but soup.

'Just "all right"? These are some of the best mushrooms in the province! They only grow in one place and I'm the only one who knows where they are. They taste magnificent, even better than truffles.'

'Rubbish. I could pick a kilo tomorrow in about ten minutes in the back garden of my wife's house in the country. They're as common as field mushrooms. Come on, how much do you want for these dried-out little specimens?'

'1,000 pesetas a kilo?' His tone was unconvincing.

'1,000? Ludicrous. Do you think I'm going to spend that kind of money on buying a few kilos of earth? Look at this one. You've brought half the forest with it.' They haggled and argued until they finally reached a price. Pedro wrote him out a note and sent him up to Duque to receive his cash payment. Pedro turned to me in triumph. 'These are some of the finest mushrooms you can get. The only way to prepare them is *a la plancha* – grilled on the hot plate – sprinkled with salt, parsley and a little diced jamón serrano. Any other way would detract from the taste.' The mushroom man came back down the stairs happy. He had got what he wanted – instant cash and both bags sold at once. Pedro invited him to have a drink of wine. He declined the offer but reached out to shake Pedro's hand with a broad smile stretching across his lined and ruddy face.

'You are a one, you know, Carabias. You're smarter than a rabbit. Anyway, love to the family. We part in peace.'

Two or three times I had tried to get hold of Tomás Urrialde to go mushroom picking with him, but he had been away for the last six months doing a lecture tour of Latin America. So I took up María del Mar's offer of going to the pine woods with her instead. It might not be as informative but I would learn some eccentric country customs.

We went out to María del Mar's village, on the edge of the sierra, early on a Saturday morning. She was already up and working in her walled garden. Suspended six feet up in the air from the tops of the fruit trees were four life-size scarecrows. She had gone to extraordinary lengths to make them realistic. One of them had a pair of laddered tights and shoes, another a white plastic handbag; and the largest of all had a see-through net shopping bag with empty tins of mussels and a jumbo-size packet of Persil.

She was very pleased to see us. We had come in time to see her finishing off a pagan fertility rite. The fruit crop had been minimal this year.

'We are too near to the sierra and the late frosts have damaged the blossoms. The scarecrows have been redundant this year.' She was thinking of buying them wigs. Next year all would be better and the branches would be weighed down with fruit. She was going to make sure this time. She took a long piece of rope out of the corpse of the first car they had ever owned, which doubled as a greenhouse, and patiently unravelled it.

She fetched an old tin bucket and filled it from the well. Next, she grabbed a heavy rock, tied one end of the rope around it and lowered it into the bucket. Could I help her, reach up as high as possible and tie the other end of the rope around the trunk of one of the pears? I tied a tight knot and she walked away with the bucket until the rope was taut. She set it down on the ground. 'That should do it. Next year will be a bumper crop.' How was this device going to help? It was pointless to ask. María del Mar's reasoning powers and sense of logic defeated all attempts at analysis.

María del Mar always wore an apron with deep, catch-all pockets. They were full of useless items which she always found a use for: half a clothes-peg, bottle tops, acorns, a spark plug, a teacup handle –anything she had encountered on her twenty-mile rambles. Later they might come in useful. How? Well... she knitted her brow and became very pensive. How could you possibly find the solution if you didn't yet know the problem?

A car horn sounded at the other end of the village.

'Do you want to come with me?' she asked. 'It's the bread man.' 'That's good,' said Alex, 'a door-to-door service. It's not so isolated in the village after all. How often does he come?' she asked Marie de Mar. 'Every three days. On the first day he comes on the second day he doesn't and on the third day he comes again. Every three days. It's not often enough really, because Paco loves his bread. He eats a loaf with each meal.'

After fetching the bread María del Mar was ready for our expedition. Before going up into the pine forests, however, we would have to go down to the other end of the village and pick blackberries, before the Madrid weekenders stole them all. She fetched two old oil cans and strode out into the street, followed at arm's length by her two mongrel dogs. She slipped on her green crochet beret. María del Mar was round about fifty and when young she must have been a strikingly beautiful woman. She had sea-green, luminous eyes that sparkled with mischief. She never missed a thing.

Did I mind moving my car from in front of the giant garage doors, because it might be in the way? she requested politely. Her son had phoned from Barcelona last week and he had promised to come and visit them some time before Christmas. She hadn't seen him since Corpus Christi at the beginning of the summer. If he came while we were up on the hill collecting mushrooms he wouldn't be able to get his new car into the garage. I didn't have to move it far, just a few feet.

If I hadn't met her myself I wouldn't have thought her possible. However mad she sounded, she was far from being mentally disturbed. It was just that she had inherited and maintained many of the age-old country habits and customs. If some of them were only half-remembered, her imagination took over and filled in the missing parts of the puzzle.

We collected enough blackberries to make jam and then headed up into the hills for mushrooms. She burrowed into her pockets and took out a handful of raw acorns and offered us some. They were full of energy, she said. I tried one, in case I had been missing some delectable gastronomic treat. I instantly spat it out when she wasn't looking but the dogs gave me away. It was too bitter for my liking, I told her.

The woods were beautiful. The mixture of vegetation, from scrub oak to hollies, beech, silver birch and pine, extended through the full range of earth colours. As the sunlight hit the leaves the woods transformed themselves into something magical. This was where the wild boar fed when the snows covered the mountain. Below us we could hear the sound of the river running along its course. It was one of their favourite haunts, María del Mar told us. They came down here for drinking water and acorns but after next Sunday when the big-game season opened they would escape back up into the mountains. Paco loved hunting and was a member of the village shoot. It annoyed her. He was a plasterer by trade and her living room was still unfinished three years after he'd started the job. When he wasn't transforming someone else's house into a model interior he was up and away out on the hills. He didn't have any other vices, like smoking or drinking, but she had resigned herself to his never finishing it.

María del Mar had an intense look of concentration on her face.

'There's a mushroom,' she said, pointing a few feet away. I couldn't see a thing. She bent over and lifted up a layer of pine needles, and there it was, a deep orange niscalo – *lactarius deliciosus*. She popped it into her apron. The same thing happened again and again with increasing frequency. Apart from all her other skills, did María del Mar also have X-ray eyes? I studied her movements carefully and succeeded in uprooting the odd niscalo myself. It was a simple trick. The same rain that had fed the mushrooms had also squashed the bed of pine needles flat. If you bent down low and looked a few feet ahead of you the raking light threw the swelling mound partly into shade. By the end of the morning we had collected ten kilos of niscalos, enough to last us through the winter. María del Mar had also uprooted a selection of weeds that she was going to use for home cures of various different ailments. I was convinced that she must be a *curandera* – a cross between a witchdoctor and a faith healer. In the villages they were still quite common. If anyone fell ill they would first go to see the village doctor but as often as not they didn't trust the doctor's diagnosis. The curandero would then be called in. One morning in Segovia I had seen Paco searching through the undergrowth on the banks of the river Clamores. Someone in his family was suffering from kidney stones and he was looking for a particular kind of thistle that would cure them, boiled up with water and drunk every few hours over a period of a week. The kidney stones would simply disappear.

On our way back to the village María del Mar spotted a wild bees' nest. I gave it a wide berth. Did we mind hanging around while she smoked them out and collected the honey? She pulled a jar out of her pocket.

'We haven't really got time, I'm afraid. We're expected back in Segovia any minute now.' That was a terrible pity, she said, because she had hoped we would stay for lunch.

Cooking was not María del Mar's forte. Everything was thrown into a dirty old stockpot and left for hours bubbling in the ashes of the fire but it always turned out greasy and swimming in oil. On our last visit she had given us some special chocolates her sister had made. The recipe was a simple mix of a third lard, a third cocoa powder and a third sugar. They were quite disgusting.

If we weren't going to stay and watch, she would leave the honey collecting to later on in the afternoon. A few years ago she had taught some stupid city people from Madrid how to collect the honey but they got everything wrong and were all badly stung. We waved her goodbye. 'Come out next weekend, if you want to, we're slaughtering the family pig and making chorizos.'

Traditional pig killing was coming back into fashion again. In the fifties most of the villages around Segovia had become almost completely depopulated when necessity and ambition had forced people into the cities to look for work. But as a result of the economic boom of the last few years weekenders had returned to their villages and were discovering their roots. Antique shops and those specializing in homemade produce were flourishing. Nostalgia had become a profitable business and some of the restaurants cashed in by staging pig-killing displays in front of the restaurant. It was a gruesome show but it had a good following.

At one of these I had overheard a man describe the scene with the kind of terminology normally reserved for bull-fighting: 'That was a beautiful, clean kill.' Afterwards everyone would go into the restaurant and tuck into a gigantic pork banquet.

'There's nothing to be squeamish about,' said Pedro. Near his wife's village there was a matador who slaughtered pigs every Thursday. I should go and have a look. So the following Thursday, a crisp and sunny November morning, I drove down to meet Chencho the Matador. It was still warm enough in the sun to wear only a shirt and a thin jumper.

Chencho was a short and corpulent character, who reminded me of Chaucer's Miller. His face had been blasted a livid red by a mixture of the wind, sun and alcohol. The veins on his bulbous nose had burst. He had taken his car out of the garage which doubled as the slaughterhouse. The pigs hadn't arrived yet. His assistants were out collecting them in his van. There would be six pigs today, which meant a full day's work.

Chencho's slaughterhouse was a professional outfit but it didn't have air-conditioning, so he could only work from November through to early April. It had to be cold enough so that the meat didn't spoil. The large multinationals which owned the chorizo and wind-dried ham factories in Segovia worked all the year through. But Chencho was just a slaughterer, and his clients from the villages would later come to collect the meat and finish off all the different preparations in their own homes.

The van came rolling down the hill. His assistants were the two village dairymen and the shepherd who worked alongside Chencho every Thursday morning to earn some extra cash. The slaughter bench was brought out and placed in the forecourt. The van was stationary but rocked from side to side with the cavortings of its occupants. I stood and watched.

On the other side of the road we had been joined by some other spectators, the Guardia Civil – the rural police, who stayed seated in their car. They were there to check that Chencho wasn't killing more pigs than had been registered with the vet. Or perhaps they had been given a tip-off; maybe Chencho had been 'denounced' by a rival village butcher. They didn't seem to worry him.

Every pig killed in Spain has to be tested for trichonosis and African swine fever. The latter was the most worrying as it would spread like the plague and the herd would have to be destroyed. In most areas of Spain it had been totally eradicated, and Segovia province, where more than a million pigs were slaughtered every year, had its last recorded case more than five years ago. It was one of the conditions for export to the EEC, but this batch wasn't travelling far, it was purely for home consumption. One pig would feed the average peasant family for most of the year. All other meats consumed were regarded as a luxury.

The shepherd picked up a billy-hook and went in the back door of the van, which was closed behind him. The noise was dreadful and the van swayed crazily from side to side. The shepherd banged on the side and shouted for us to open the door, and he came out backwards dragging a screaming and kicking beast into the sun. He had hooked it under the chin and it was putting up a fight. The other three men surrounded it and pushed it towards the bench. It was a large animal, weighing close to 100 kilos. I preferred to remain a spectator.

They lifted it on the bench and tied it down fast on its side. The men themselves were almost caricatures: the fat, the thin, the tall and the short. The Guardia Civil looked on expressionless and bored (perhaps they took me for the vet). The top foreleg of the animal was left unattached and free. Chencho's wife brought out a large earthenware bowl and placed it on the ground near the neck of the pig. She was going to use the blood to make blood cake and spicy morcilla. Chencho sharpened his knife on a steel and set to work. All of the men held the pig down tight as Chencho located the artery and stabbed in the blade. The screaming was horrendous but I tried not to feel sorry. I loved chorizo and ham, and wasn't about to give them up. It would have been hypocritical to accuse the men of cruelty. It was, if you looked at it in context, the most natural of scenes.

The blood came gushing out into the bowl and after a minute the animal became quiet. Chencho shouted to his assistants to hold it tighter, and pumped up and down with the free leg. For the final few seconds the pig convulsed and jerked wildly in its death throes, and it was all over. This scene repeated itself another five times, and throughout the men laughed and joked as they set to their work. It wasn't out of embarrassment, because what they were doing must have been as normal to them as buttering toast.

The fourth of the pigs had proved a problem. The shepherd hadn't tied it down tight. In its death throes it had escaped and kicked over the earthenware crock of blood. I was standing ten yards away and my jumper was spattered. The tall dairyman was the closest to the scene and he was covered from head to toe. When it was over they stood back and lit their cigarettes. Chencho pointed to the bloody dairyman and joked to me:

'Just like a Christ! Don't you think?' He brooded over it. 'Yes, just like a Christ.' The leftovers of the blood were thrown to the village dogs, and the Guardia's car started up and disappeared over the hill. Chencho's partners moved off as well and he was left to the time-consuming job of dealing with the dead pigs.

From his barn he fetched a straw bale and dragged one of them into the centre of the concrete forecourt. It was turned on its back and was covered completely under a mound of straw. Chencho lit it and the flames leapt up ten feet. He picked up a sheaf of burning straw and worked around the body where the fire had missed it. Next he picked up a small wooden block on to which he had nailed bottle tops with their serrated edges sticking forwards. When the fire had died down, he scraped the skin with this implement and washed the pig carefully with water from a hose. The next stage was to eviscerate the carcass, so I thought I'd leave him to it and go back to Duque's.

'Was it good?' asked Santos. 'Good' didn't seem to be quite the right word to describe what I had just seen.

'Today,' said Pedro, 'we are going to prepare a month's supply of *chorizo en olla*. Remember, Gisbert,' – Pedro winked at me – '*el mejor injección – chorizo y jamón* (the best injection – chorizo and ham).' The government hadn't used this as a slogan in their anti-drugs campaigns but I was sure they must have toyed with the idea. Chorizo is a drug in itself. The flavour of the paprika is addictive and just one piece of chorizo in a stew transforms it completely. Chorizo en olla is my favourite way of preparing a large quantity of freshly made chorizo. Some people just hang them up in their cool larder for a month to dry but it sometimes ends up tough and in the summer this method gives varied results.

5 kg fresh chorizo *2 litres good olive oil*
Large preserving pan
Sterilised wide-necked preserving jars

Pour the olive oil in the pan. Chop up the chorizo into two-inch lengths (enough for a sandwich or a small tapa). Add the chorizo to the oil and heat up slowly. Initially the oil will only come halfway up the mound of chorizo but as the chorizo begins to lose its fat, and the oil changes colour with the paprika, it will cover everything. Turn the chorizo every ten minutes and make sure that the oil does not fry the meat. After roughly an hour turn off the heat. Using tongs, carefully fill the storage jars with the shrunken chorizo lengths and pour in the oil to cover. (It is worth remembering that the oil will stay burning hot for hours depending on the quantity. Handle the full storage jars with care and prepare the dish away from small children.) Seal the jars and store somewhere cool. It will keep for months if you ensure that the meat always remains covered. The oil and fat mixture can be used for frying and flavouring other dishes.

Pedro had received an invitation from a friend who ran a restaurant in Burgo de Osma, two and a half hours east of Segovia, to go to a banquet. He couldn't go, but would I like to go along with Alex instead? The Hotel-Restaurant Virrey Palafox is famous right across Spain. People fly in from Seville and Barcelona just to eat one of their pig banquets. He showed me the programme of events. Next weekend would be the best, as they were concentrating on the hams of Jabugo. This tiny village in Andalucía still makes hams from the wild black Iberian pigs that have been fattened up on acorns and walnuts. As it cost anything up to £35 a pound I had still never tried it.

We set off early on Saturday morning. The festivities were going to start at noon. The drive to Burgo de Osma was beautiful. On our right hand side the sierra was in sight almost all the way. The sunflowers had been burnt black by the sun, left to dry on their stalks. It looked as if a forest fire had swept across the fields. Just outside Riaza a family of wild boar ran across the road – a mother with her litter of five young. They stopped for a brief moment to look, then charged away into the low scrub for safety. Smoke was billowing out of the chimneys as we passed through the villages. This was the main road across this part of Spain, running from Extremadura in the West to the Mediterranean and Catalonia; we saw maybe a dozen other cars.

We arrived at the Virrey Palafox, and the owner straight-away invited us to an aperitif of Martini and soda. My wife might need it, he joked, because they were going to slaughter a pig in the forecourt of the hotel to kick off the festivities. He introduced us to our fellow lunch guest, Federico, 'cultural attaché' of Jabugo, a strange-looking man. But first to the pig killing. It was no different from Chencho's performance, except that it was played out in front of a crowd close to a thousand strong. Whole families had come to witness the spectacle. Little children were held high on their parents' shoulders to get a better view. They looked on, transfixed.

After the pig had been despatched we were requested to join the procession, in Federico's honour. Two dulzaina players and a drummer led the way across to Burgo's town-hall. The Mayor was there to meet us and invited us into the council chamber. It was time for the speeches and the receiving of gifts. Federico, like his more famous namesake García Lorca, was a poet, and he had come to sing the praises of Jabugo ham. He reminded me of a Segovian poet I had met who had just published his first work of poems dedicated to the slaughter of pigs. Burgo's Mayor hoped that Federico would return to his village and also sing the praises of Castillian pork products. Gifts were exchanged. Federico took his presents out of a plastic bag: two pieces of porcelain sculpture which had broken on the journey. It didn't matter. He gave them anyway. He showed the Mayor where the pieces should be stuck on and we went off to the banquet.

In a gigantic hall we were shown to our table. Federico was placed opposite me and the owner took the head of the table. It was going to be jolly, no question. I could see already from the hundreds of other diners that they had come here for fun. The owner tied a bib round our necks and called out for our food. Ahead lay a fifteen-course pork marathon, accompanied by white, red and rosé wines, with champagne and liqueurs to finish. The dulzaina struck up and the clapping started. I looked across at Federico and was convinced that this overweight dandy was wearing mascara. His fat fingers tapered off into long and polished fingernails. Perhaps a flamenco guitarist as well? He slipped off his tight-fitting jacket and retied his bib. He was going to attack the meal with gusto, part of his diplomatic mission.

Our first dishes consisted of the cured meats of his village: hams, chorizos and wind-dried tenderloins – *lomos*. This was followed by black pudding, a soup, pasties with pork, cochinillo, pork chops, stews, marinaded pork fillets, pork and prunes, kidneys and a salad of pigs' ears with strawberries.

The owner was anxious that Federico should enjoy himself.

'Did you enjoy that, Federico?'

'Yes, very good.' Before Federico could stop him another repeat order was called out for – 'for the poet from the south'. He ate twice as much as I did and I could barely walk. The buttons on his shirt came undone. As we passed from wine to wine, Federico poured the remainder of whatever was in his glass into a carafe. The crowds were getting rowdy; singing and dancing began. Federico looked pleased with the performance and sweated profusely. His bib did good service and the carafe of cast-offs was beginning to fill. For a poet, he spoke very little. He had little time between mouthfuls: good tactics – that way at least his grunts of approval could be read with sufficient ambiguity. 'Did you enjoy that?' – followed by a grunt could mean anything from excellent to so-so.

Ten dishes into the banquet his main concern had switched from diplomacy to self-preservation. About the only thing that was still keeping his shirt on was the florid tie around his neck. 'Was there any dish that we had particularly enjoyed?' asked the owner. I had learnt from Federico's shining, livid red example. I praised them all.

Coffee was ordered and Federico asked for a green Chartreuse chaser, to go with his carafe of cast-offs which he now obviously mistook for some rough-and-ready peasant wine. His taste buds were in rebellion but he had at least upheld the honour of his village. The dulzainista came to join us at table and asked if Federico might accompany him in song; it would crown a memorable occasion. I would have paid him to get up, but there was no budging him – he had dined himself to an utter standstill.

The following weekend we went over to see María del Mar. 'How was the *matanza* (the pig slaughtering)?' I asked. Very successful, she answered, but the pig had been so large that they had had to hold it down with the forklift of the tractor. I was glad we had missed it.

'Tomorrow there's a wild-boar hunt. I'm sure if you ask the shepherd he'll take you along. He's famous around the provinces. He kills them by hand.' I had learnt to take most of María del Mar's claims lightly, but this one was so outrageous I decided to check up. Outrageously, it was true. He had brought two wild boar down from the hills only last week. He travelled with a twelve-bore shotgun but the art was to track the beast down with the help of the dogs and stab it through the heart with a hand-knife. I was invited along.

The village shoot met early the following morning. They had swapped their normal shoot for one over in the foothills of Ávila, an hour away. I had often seen hunters in full green costume waiting outside Cándido's on weekend mornings and that was where we had arranged to pick up the remaining hunters as we passed through. The shepherd loaded his motley pack of dogs into his van and off we went the fifteen dogs lying peacefully in the back. We reached the large, sweeping estate by nine o'clock and the first hour was spent talking through the plans for the morning, the placement of the guns – and eating a sack of churros, helped down by a weak rosé drunk straight from the pig's bladder. The shepherd, his dogs and I waited while the guns went out and took up their positions. He hoped we would have luck but it was unlikely today. There was still not enough snow to force them off the mountains. Naturally, he didn't know the lie of the land as well as he did the terrain surrounding his village, but it was always possible that a few families had found peaceful reserves close to a spring. Were they regarded as a pest? I asked him.

'Not a pest, but they can do a lot of damage. They love the taste of sunflowers and a family of wild boar can wreak havoc in a single night. They eat cabbages too and go through the rubbish bins. Last week in Riaza a Frenchman had his whole experimental truffle farm rooted up. Sometimes they break into the pig enclosures and couple with the sows. Hombre, it's not so bad but it costs a fortune in fencing.'

The time had come for the shepherd, his dogs and I to start broad sweeps across the estate. We were the beaters. He shouted orders to the dogs continuously and told me to shout out every half a minute or so, so the guns would be able to locate us. My worry wasn't the guns but the chance that the dogs might circle and pen in a boar. If this happened, the shepherd said he would have to go in. Shooting was too dangerous and it might kill one of his pack. The knife on his belt was the only answer. I swallowed hard. They were dangerous, weren't they?

'The tusks are razor sharp. They can cut through your leg straight down to the bone. You wouldn't even notice.' Oh no? I looked around for a tree large enough to shin up, but we were surrounded by shrub.

The shepherd was like a Red Indian tracker. He stopped and smelt. We lit up cigarettes and waited. He listened. Nothing. He kicked a divot in the ground and buried his cigarette stub. He looked thoughtful as if he might have caught the scent.

'The trouble is, you know, it's always us shepherds that get the blame. Every summer there are forest fires and the public always imagine it's us who have started them. It's hard enough to find feed at the best of times. Do you think I'm then going to go and burn it all down? It's ridiculous. I always dig a hole and bury the stub. It wouldn't matter now after all the rains, but it's my habit. It's the picnic people from Madrid who do it. They leave their broken bottles and forget to put out their barbecues.' He looked across at a small scrub oak. A patch of fresh earth had been turned, right under its trunk. 'The wild boar have been here within the last hour. The droppings are still warm.' He reached for a branch that had been stripped away with rubbing and picked off a hair. 'A three-year-old female.' From down in the valley we could hear shouts go up and echo across the hill. Seconds later there were three shots from a gun. The message was shouted up to us on the ridge like Chinese whispers. A fox! 'Good. The boar might still be about.' My heart leapt up into my throat. 'They're like pheasant. They bury themselves in.' He shouted out orders to his roving pack of dogs. 'But once you burrow them out it's like an explosion. They're faster than hare.' I was having kittens.

I had got myself in and there was no going back. I stuck close to the shepherd and observed him closely. He was wiry and strong. He had been in this position maybe a thousand times before. It gave me confidence. One of the dogs let loose a frightening howl. The pack ran off with the shepherd behind. I followed at a discreet distance, keeping him in my sights. The shepherd shouted back to me.

'Come on. It's more dangerous there. They sometimes turn in the panic and break through the pack. That's when they're the most dangerous.' The howls tailed off when the dogs lost the scent. From down in the valley the cries came up again. A fox! And the shots rang out.

We zigzagged across the estate all morning but there was nothing to be had. We regrouped at the cars and ate chorizo and tortilla bocadillos. No one had seen a boar and the total bag for the day was three foxes and a rabbit. It was time to drive back to Segovia for the shoot lunch in the village schoolroom. Did I want to come out in the afternoon for an unofficial shoot in the hills above the village? No, thank you. That afternoon they took three boar.

AQUEDUCT AT SEGOVIA.

12: Christmas

Families celebrate Christmas throughout the Segovian province and the capital in the same way. The part of the ritual starts late in November with the buying of the lottery tickets for the special Christmas draw. But the buying is only the first part of this complicated transaction. In lotteries the odds are always stacked heavily against the participants becoming instant millionnaires. There is a way, however, it seems, of trying to lessen the odds and that is by swapping tickets with the fishmonger, the butcher, cousins in Madrid, uncles in Seville, a taxi driver who may have swapped it with someone from the Canary Islands. The principle behind it is that there is only so much luck a city the size of Segovia can be expected to enjoy. If you spread the load between various cities your five tickets somehow count for more. It's a kind of tactical voting: the perverse philosophy of the ever-hopeful gambler. Even more optimistic are the official lottery stalls which put up a big sign saying that they won last week's 'fat' one, with the idea of advertising their success. It seems to me the gambling equivalent of closing the stable door once the horse has bolted.

Having bought tickets early on in the month does not, however, disqualify the purchaser from further investment, or even upgrading or downgrading the tickets. Lottery tickets are always kept on one's person in case the opportunity arises. For the last few days before Christmas they are almost worth their weight in gold.

The next traditional purchase which will last for the whole fiesta period, leading up to Three Kings on the sixth of January, are the bars of *turrón*: thick bars of nougat, chocolate, chopped almonds and dried fruits in all their possible permutations. Cut up into blocks and put out on the best silver tray, they are pulled out of the cupboard for every visitor to the house to nibble on.

Then of course there are the presents but fortunately the full fervour of advertising hype has still not hit Segovia, so buying is not an obsessive activity from September on. Better still, the Christmas lights only come on a few days before Christmas when the electricity company, it is rumoured, has finally got the council to settle the previous year's account. This year for the first time the Caja de Ahorros, the local savings bank, decided to make a gesture towards a northern European Christmas and mounted a giant pine in the square just down from the aqueduct. Three Kings, which always used to be the festival day when the children received their presents, has now been firmly replaced by Christmas Day. Slowly, but surely (not wishing to sound overly nostalgic for a tradition that has never been mine), old ways are disappearing to be replaced by toned-down uniformity.

At least the traditional Christmas foods have remained intact: mounds of the most expensive and exotic shellfish, baby elvers spiked with red-hot peppers and burnt garlic, red bream in an orange sauce, stewed hen, figs and all those fruits preserved in chinchón and aguardiente. Which makes me think of the prizewinning recipe that José ('Pepe') Martín at Las Columnas promised to pass onto me for stewed hen – *gallina en pepitoria* (literally 'hen in a hotchpotch').

Pepe had won Young Segovian Chef-of-the-Year with this test recipe. It is a relatively sophisticated and rich preparation of what is a cheap, basic ingredient – chicken. Chicken is for home cooking and is definitely not a Christmas treat. In the bars and restaurants of Madrid and Segovia pollo en pepitoria is served as a menu-of-the-day standard, a dish that Pedro and Mariano would prepare for the rest of the staff once a week.

If chicken isn't good enough, then a hen specially fattened up is. In the villages north of Segovia, out on the meseta, the peasants slaughter one of the family hens to prepare the dish on Christmas Eve – *Nochebuena*. With all the family together, it takes its place as the centre of the feast. After a few slices of chorizo, the first course is a rice dish, similar to paella, which uses up the remaining *menudillos* (offal): gizzards, winglets, necks and kidneys. After finishing the gallina en pepitoria and sopping up the last of the sauce with bread, they go on to eat grapes which have been hanging from the wooden beams as decoration since the harvest.

Pepe showed me how to make the dish under the watchful eye of his father Primitivo, a chef who had trained at Cándido's alongside Pedro Carabias and Tomás Urrialde, the Mushroom Man. While Pepe was preparing his version for me – which included apple in the *picada* – a voice shouted up from the street, asking what was para familia today. Minutes later the butcher in his traditional horizontally striped green and black apron was in the kitchen, waiting impatiently for his little taster.

Watching the pot keenly he whispered his proposal to Marie Angeles, a washing-up girl, and promised she would never be without fillet steak on her plate. Blushing, she turned away as his finger went in the pot.

1½ kg chicken or hen
2 tbsp olive oil
Water
Half litre dry white wine
1 bay leaf
Half litre chicken stock
Salt, nutmeg, white pepper, flour to dust

For the picada:

1 head of garlic
1 pinch of saffron
50 g blanched almonds
50 g pine nuts
1 boiled egg yolk
1 chicken liver
1 tbsp chopped parsley
1 slice fried bread
1 glass dry white wine
2 tbsp olive oil
1 onion, finely diced
2 cloves garlic, finely diced
1 tbsp flour
1 cored apple
1 clove:
1 glass fino sherry

For the garnish:

1 chopped egg yolk and 2 whites
1 tbsp chopped parsley
1 tbsp chopped almonds

Joint the chicken. Remove legs and wings. Cut down breast bone and chop into eight pieces. Reserve liver. Sprinkle chicken pieces with salt, ground nutmeg and white pepper. Dust with flour. Fry in olive oil till golden. Add white wine, chicken stock, bay leaf and add water to cover. Bring to boil and simmer. Prepare picada. Crush garlic cloves until smooth. Add saffron, blanched almonds and pine nuts. Work in pestle and mortar until a smooth paste. Crumble egg yolk, fried chicken liver, clove, parsley and fried bread into the mortar. Cut apple into small pieces, having skinned and cored it. Add sherry and white wine. Work until smooth. Add to chicken in the casserole.

Fry onion and garlic in the olive oil until transparent. Add flour and stir until smooth. Pour into casserole through a sieve. Stir. Simmer chicken for one hour, three hours or more for hen. Lay chicken out on serving dish, spoon over sauce and garnish.

Serve with white rice, mashed potato, or bread.

By midway through the month the shopping begins to get feverish. Boni and Sagrario would be catering for all the Madrid relations, and there were thirty or so presents to buy. Children expected presents on both Christmas Day and Three Kings. Boni thought it excessive. She remembered the Civil War and the Hunger Years. In those times she would have been lucky to get a single present; now everything was so 'exaggerated' (a favourite word). The children wanted everything and life was hell if they didn't get it. Where had all the greed come from? Television! She didn't agree with it, but she would indulge her grandchildren all the same. It wasn't the time for denying them joy, was it? When they got older there was plenty of time to learn.

I walked up calle Réal to say my farewells to Pedro, Mariano, the Duques and all the other staff. I hadn't warned them – I felt it was best that way. On the street the beggars were out again for the first time since the summer, gambling on Christmas charity. It was cold and miserable, and the fur coats were on show.

'So you're leaving us,' said Pedro. 'You won't stay away for long. Segovia doesn't give up its prisoners that easily. You'll be back.' And he said it with such certainty that we both knew it was true.

Jai, at La Concha, told me the same. Fate had brought me here. As I became more experienced I would catch the Segovian boredom, complain about the bureaucracy, rail against provincialism, become complacent – but leave? Never. I couldn't possibly live again without so much beauty.

'You'll try but you won't succeed,' said Jai.

My head was quarrelling but my heart agreed.

13: Epilogue

Jai was right. We couldn't get Segovia out of our blood. It has dug its way in deep.

Just before we returned back to England we acquired an old farmhouse cum village bar, telephone kiosk and mayor's office – all under one roof – so that we would never lose touch with our beloved city. It was our foothold. A staging post that linked our future and our past. And it would change our view of the city forever.

Friendships have endured and over the years become far more profound. Family meals now include our three children and a host of their friends from their village club, the Peña de los Rebeldes. Coffee is served forth to our friends from the various village tribes: Calixto and Nieves, the family of Martín and Sevi and Avito, amongst many others.

A relaxed six hour meal with the 'A' team, the 'Equipo' – Angel, Teresa, Caché, Lara, Vicky, Julio, Pilar, Angulo, Joy, Fernando, Matilde, Cruz, Nieves, Luis, Carmen, Diego, Ana, Tom, Rebecca, José María, Leo, Jai, Gloria, Eva, los Lobos, Victor, Cristina, Sara, Marta, Mark 'Caveman', Miguel Angel, Gema, Tonio and all the Poguntkes – means preparing a selection of dishes for thirty or more. For the village friends in Arevalillo de Cega, who now feel more like family, I bring coals to Newcastle and serve forth an extensive range of dishes for a typical Vino Español – tapas and wine. My time with Pedro Carabias has served me well.

Inevitably, much has changed in the decade since I first wrote this book. The chance of spotting a Castilian peasant on his faithful mule has all but gone. Even less likely, the odd viewing of his wife aboard a threshing plank circling endlessly around – protected from the sun by a clumsy folded hat, fashioned from last week's newspaper. Many villages and towns have been completely transformed. Even the grandeur and the tough psychological reality of the harsh Castilian countryside has been tamed by the Garden Centre and the new cult of the country. New motorways cut a swathe through the barren wastes of the meseta plain bringing neighbouring cities closer together.

But despite the arrival of new wealth and upmarket sophistication, it remains just a thin veneer, barely covering the sustaining values that lie hidden deep in the Castilian soul. A distance of ten years has now finally made everything clear.

Our moment in Segovia, captured in this book, proved a magical time – in fact, almost stolen from time. We didn't recognise it then, but there in the mid 1980's we had arrived in the city of Segovia right at the tail end of all that explosive energy and enthusiasm encapsulated by the movement known as the Madrid 'movida', captured forever in the films by Pedro Almodovar. Being a provincial city Segovia caught 'la movida's' infectious and seductive sense of rebellion late on in the day. But caught it we did. Liberty, free flowing political exchange, love, late nights, laughter and a huge sense of optimism – with its concomitant 'boom' and rising property prices – fuelled us as we approached that almost mythical year of 1992.

Tom and I dreamed and fantasised about our glorious futures in Segovia. And in this we weren't unusual. Anything seemed possible. However, the reality of living in two clapped out farmhouses, plagued by mosquitos and carpeted with sheep droppings, made for many a comic interlude.

In 1991, presumably as an indication of how quickly Spain was transforming itself into a wealthy modern European state, I was requested to review the 3 star Michelin restaurant Zalacain, in central Madrid, for the American publication Town and Country. Following our ablutions – outdoor showers in 10 below zero – Tom and I dutifully ironed our trousers with a damp cloth folded around a heated brick, fashioned cufflinks from discarded paper clips and then feasted a few hours later rather incongruously on the smoothest of foie-gras, spiked with pungent truffles from Guadalajara, followed by a pickled partridge escabeche in a 40 year old vintage sherry vinegar, and dishes of wafer thin slices of jamón iberico, cut deliberately from the back left leg of the black acorn-fed wild Iberian pig – the back left, according to folklore, the most tender part of the beast following years of porcine reverie while dozing on this favoured left haunch. All this, quite naturally, was washed down with liberal quantities of Tanqueray Gin and tonic, crisp white Ruedas, majestic Pesquera wines and deep mahogany-toned brandies from rare barrels hidden away in exclusive bodegas in southern Jerez, belonging to the Lustaus. We returned to our peaceful valley satisfied and sated, triumphant in the knowledge that we had given of our best and feasted like lords.

But the hangover and reality were bound to hit soon – just as night follows day and just as Lent follows hard on Carnival's heel. This much I had learnt from my first encounter with the legendary text *The Book of Good Love* – a mediaeval morality manual punctuated liberally with gastronomic feasts and the pleasures of sex – written by a 14th century priest, the Archpriest of Hita, Juan Ruiz and set in the foothills of Segovia and the Guadarrama range.

The first victim to this colder more measured gaze was the careful wiping away of the multitude of layers of romantic patina with which we had painted 'our' city. Segovia remains beautiful. Bewitching. But life moves on.

Nostalgia apart, the dramatic changes in Segovia over the last decade have been managed quite well. After all, the aqueduct is still standing, say the Segovian wags. A small triumph. But there are losses to Segovian gastronomy that seem to mark the passing of an age. Within a couple of years both Cándido Lopez and Dionisio Duque died. Their passing represented a rupture with the classical culinary past and the arrival of new ingredients and new techniques.

On a personal level, sadder still, was the untimely death of María del Mar who taught me so much about village folklore but whose skills as a 'curendera' – faith healer – failed her at the last. In Valseca , a village nearby, Felipa the Rosquillera – the biscuit lady – with her powerful forearms that moulded and pounded the dough patiently for hours slowly withered away – a folk recipe and technique that had beguiled Presidents and Kings sadly died with her.

On a more cheerful note it is gratifying that many of my earliest predictions as to the rising stars of Castilian gastronomy – no doubt suggested to me by Pedro Carabias, Nicolas and Jai – proved almost always right. The Martín family left Bar Columnas and then set up a hugely successful temple to game cooking, La Matita in nearby Collado Hermoso. Nicolas continues to put many a Michelin starred chef to shame with his exquisite banquets in the basement of La Concepción. José María and Tomás Postigo with their Pago de Carrovejas red wine – after a string of medals and prestigious international awards – have been chosen as one of the fifty top bodegas in the entire world with the greatest future in the coming millennium. Alejandro Fernandez, at Pesquera, is up somewhere in the stratosphere, as generous as ever and as passionate as always about his heavenly wine. Mariano Garcia has left Vega Sicilia to head Mauro, and will no doubt create another string of masterpieces that will drink without compare. On a more humble level, the bakery in Matamala still bakes the most extraordinarily moreish cartwheel size loaves of bread – with their slight crusty sourness. Artisan goats cheeses are arriving from the village of Sacramenia accompanied by a ewe's milk junket that trembles in anticipation for the first dig of the spoon. The Venta Pinillos still fry the best plate of chorizo and eggs. Mazaka's tortillas in the La Granja market bar – creamy soft and yellow – are still some of the best – as too is his wine buying advice. Chafa's seafood is difficult to fault and Zaca's escabeche of partridge remains a dish fit for a king.

Ten years on... what else has changed? The peseta has gone and the euro is in. To see an off-duty policeman with a brandy in hand is a thing of the dim and distant past... -30ºC or not. The breathalyser is now the most frequently used piece of police kit.

El Alcázar, the patisserie shop on the plaza, has had its secrecy and suspiciousness rewarded with a full patent on the legendary pudding, Ponche Segoviano. 'Tinin', Zute El Mayor, the master roaster of milk-fed lambs from nearby Sepulveda, has quite deservedly won the Order of the Silver Chickpea.

Closer to home, Caché has reopened Peli's old house and exchanged painful and poignant memories for the laughter of children. Wild screams echo across the valley to the Vera Cruz and the monastery of El Parral as children leap into the babbling rock pool in that most privileged of urban hideaways. Gone the garlic but never the scents and smells.

Most remarkable of all, friend Lucio del Campo, the pony-tailed patron of Las Cuevas de San Estebán – the first Segovian restaurant we ever ate in – has become the Master Sommelier's champion Master Sommelier and will be known for eternity as the legendary Golden Nose of Spain. Lucio first realised he had a special gift as a five year old on his mother's arm, parading the paseo up the calle Réal, when he recognised every woman by her particular perfume and smell. 'Mrs. Chanel has just passed by with her spinster sister Miss O de Cologne.' With his photographic olfactory he can pinpoint almost every wine produced in

Spain, reserva, crianza and even the year. Thankfully, Lucio's lentil soup and his thyme stewed rabbit remain the foundation stones of his pursuit to recapture some of the age-old and often forgotten Castilian tastes.

And there are other new stars on the plaza. A new style of Castilian cooking. At its best the new style mixes the old respect for depth of taste ,that could come from nowhere else but the heartland of Castile, with a new respect for sourcing the best primary materials and a greater subtlety in presentation and appreciation for the new dietary concerns. ' Laly', Eulalio whose Restaurant Villena, on the site where Isabel was crowned Queen of Castile, hits these high notes more often than most. And, it is a truly Segovian trait that Laly continues to use the old suppliers that I encountered first more than fifteen years ago. Not the shopkeepers or the owners of the gourmet palaces, those seductive 'ultramarinos' but the retired Castilian smallholders and farmers who on a spring day might go out to collect the miniature wild watercress or come autumn root out the orange-blushed niscalo mushroom. But, on Laly's bar you will also find a bottle of the rare Pingus wine that can cost up to £700. Opened ritually for a daily supping, and served by the glass, will be Pesqueras, Emilio Moros, Teofilo Reyes, Pago de Carraovejas and other 'serious' wines from around Spain. Where has all the money come from? You may well ask. Lucky Segovia, favoured by the Romans, celebrated by the Visigoths, protected by the Moors, and recaptured by the Christians in 1085, was rewarded finally in the winter of 2000 with 'El Gordo' – the 'Fat One' – the Christmas national lottery worth more than £260 million! Food is always a central ritual in celebrating any great event. Laly, however, has steered away from vulgar displays of excess. He has refined the kitchen even more.

Most memorable of all was a 'Laly' dinner that mapped a progress through Spanish history and the arrival of new foodstuffs from across the seas. Changing fashions from country to court and from Hapsburg pomposity to contemporary minimalism were signalled as we ate crusty langouste and avocado salad, followed by iberian tenderloin of pork accompanied with peruvian purple potatoes, a light tomato reduction, and an effervescent red pepper and fava bean mousse – phantom tastes from the Americas. The final triumph was a dessert as austere and stark as any sculpture by Susana Solana – a crisp cube of featherlight puff pastry was punctured cleanly with a circular tube and filled with a warm liquid Burgos cheese custard. Placed on a lake of ebony dark chocolate it nodded its appreciation to all that is best in Spanish contemporary fashion and design as it strutted its way up the culinary catwalk.

It's a long way from the pig ear stew with which I started my Segovian apprenticeship. Or the lentils, Segovian style, that I still cook every week. But this new edition of *In the Kitchens of Castile* is I hope an honest appreciation of Castilian and Segovian food habits and rituals at a very particular moment in the city's history.

Perhaps, also now, with the demise of the tacky, utterly horrible fake 'tapas' bars dotted around London, Spanish cuisine in all its variety is finally being recognised as a world class cuisine. The writings of Elisabeth Luard, María José de Sevilla Taylor, Claudia Roden and Colman Andrews pioneered the way. But, so did Sam and Sam Clark at the wonderful Moro restaurant that picked and grazed through Andalucía, Castile and Morocco for its exciting repertoire. Most famous of all is the Catalan chef Ferrán Adria who has made crossing the Pyrenees an almost essential journey for any chef aspiring to greatness and immortality in the culinary annals of fame. But, I think, it is the victory of an essential food item that has won more converts to Spain than anything written or produced on the range. The wonderful chorizo sausage, flavoured with that deep mnemonic of paprika, has achieved final victory over the Italian salami. There is nothing quite like it. Nothing so good. Except, of course, for extra virgin olive oil from Baena in Andalucía or from the co-operative in the Catalan village of Riudoms – the Torta de Casar cheese from Extremadura – the serrano and iberico hams – and many other foodstuffs that could easily lead us on to another book.

Bridport and Arevalillo de Cega, December 2001

Cover: Segovia, Alcázar, courtesy of the
Spanish Tourist Office, London
Front cover flap: Cochinillo in Segovia, by F. Ontañon,
courtesy of the Spanish Tourist Office, London

Title page: Segovia, statue of Juan Bravo, old postcard
Half title: Segovia, Puerta de San Andrés, old postcard
All photographs collection of the author
except p. 6
Shepherd and Flock by Tom Titherington,
courtesy of the artist

Engravings by Gustave Doré, from the *Voyage en Espagne,*
various editions
except p. 46,
'El Entierro de la Sardina',
from Mesonero Romanos, *Escenas Matritense,*
Madrid 1851

If you would like further information
about titles published in the
Pallas Athene Editions series,
please write to:
Pallas Athene (Publishers) Ltd,
at the address below, or visit our website

www.pallasathene.co.uk

Series editors:
Andrew Cocks and Alexander Fyjis-Walker
Series assistants:
Della Tsiftsopoulou, Barbara Fyjis-Walker,
Madoc Threipland
Series designer:
James Sutton

First published by Sinclair-Stevenson Ltd, 1992
This edition published by Ostara Publishing
in conjunction with
Pallas Athene (Publishers) Ltd,
59 Linden Gardens,
London W2 4HJ
2003

ISBN 1 873429 04 5

Printed in Finland